A Hole in the Sidewalk

A Hole in the Sidewalk

THE RECOVERING PERSON'S GUIDE TO RELAPSE PREVENTION

Claudia Black

CRP
CENTRAL RECOVERY PRESS
LAS VEGAS

Central Recovery Press (CRP) is committed to publishing exceptional materials addressing addiction treatment, recovery, and behavioral healthcare topics.

For more information, visit www.centralrecoverypress.com.

Publisher: Central Recovery Press
            3321 N. Buffalo Drive
            Las Vegas, NV 89129

23 22   2 3 4 5

ISBN: 978-1-942094-73-9 (paper)
      978-1-942094-74-6 (e-book)

Photo of Claudia Black by Winifred Whitfield. Used with permission.

Every attempt has been made to contact copyright holders. If copyright holders have not been properly acknowledged please contact us. Central Recovery Press will be happy to rectify the omission in future printings of this book.

Publisher's Note: This book contains general information addiction and relapse prevention. The information is not medical advice and represents reference material only. This book is not a replacement for treatment from your doctor or other professional healthcare provider.

Our books represent the experiences and opinions of their authors only. Every effort has been made to ensure that events, institutions, and statistics presented in our books as facts are accurate and up-to-date. To protect their privacy, the names of some of the people, places, and institutions in this book may have been changed.

Cover and interior design by Deb Tremper, Six Penny Graphics

In honor of my friends and clients who have struggled to recover from addiction.

For many, the problem has been alcohol and other drugs; for others, gambling, food, sex, love and relationships, spending, or work. While the substance or behavior may differ, the process of the active addiction is very much the same, and relapse is common. I offer this work with respect for the insidiousness of the disease of addiction, the miracle of recovery, and the need for action.

A special thank you to Charlie Walker, Sandi Klein, and Jack Fahey. You have worked with me and supported me throughout this endeavor.

Autobiography in Five Short Chapters
Portia Nelson

I
I walk down the street.
There is a deep hole in the sidewalk.
I fall in.
I am lost . . . I am helpless.
It isn't my fault.
It takes forever to find a way out.

II
I walk down the same street.
There is a deep hole in the sidewalk.
I pretend I don't see it.
I fall in again.
I can't believe I am in the same place but it isn't my fault.
It still takes a long time to get out.

III
I walk down the same street.
There is a deep hole in the sidewalk.
I see it is there.
I still fall in . . . it's a habit.
My eyes are open. I know where I am.
It is my fault.
I get out immediately.

IV
I walk down the same street.
There is a deep hole in the sidewalk.
I walk around it.

V
I walk down another street.

Table of Contents

Preface

In nearly forty years of work in the field of addiction, I have had the honor of witnessing thousands of men and women of every age recover. Many are fortunate to remain abstinent from their first day of recovery, but there are those who relapse after several weeks, several months, or even after years of abstinence. While I have met people who have relapsed at each phase, one of my most vivid memories was of a man who had been abstinent from alcohol for thirty years. Within just three days of starting to drink again, he became so physically sick that he needed to be hospitalized. Moreover, he was as spiritually and emotionally bankrupt as he had been when he first quit three decades before. Many people die in relapse, others relapse repeatedly and chronically. Then, there are many others who relapse and return to a program of recovery and achieve continuous abstinence.

While the most prevalent form of addiction relates to alcohol and other drugs, this workbook can be utilized for a wide range of addictive disorders—from nicotine to sex, work, spending, gambling, food, and relationships. The universal component in relapse is the resumption of self-destructive behaviors. Being an addict means one is prone to relapse. To assume or simply hope it will not occur is evidence of denial. Addiction is a disease of isolation and recovery begins with connecting to others who can help you understand addiction, offer a path for recovery, and provide hope. Recovery is also about being accountable and taking action. Picking up this book is a statement that you take your addiction seriously and want to be proactive against a possible relapse. Whether or not you have a history of relapse, this book can be a major asset.

It is my hope that you are already involved in a recovery process. The single greatest contributor to relapse is losing sight of recovery as the first priority. Without recovery, everything your hold dear will be jeopardized: your health, your family, your job, your relationship with your Higher Power, and perhaps your life. If you are not involved in a recovery process, then please seek out resources in your community that can give you information as to what is available to you.

This book is not a substitute for a program of recovery. This book is an additional resource to help support your recovery.

Because people relapse at different phases in their recovery and for very different reasons, I have chosen to address a range of issues that are often overlooked or need to be reinforced. Most people will start *A Hole in the Sidewalk* from the beginning. If you choose, after you have completed the first section "Getting Started: A Look over Your Shoulder," you can skip to the subjects that you identify to be a priority. Please do not limit your responses to the numbers or lines offered. You may find it helpful to use a journal or a separate notebook. I encourage you to share what you learn about yourself with a counselor, therapist, sponsor, or recovering friend.

Depending on the form of addiction, the language that signifies recovery includes words such as clean and sober, abstinence, sobriety, etc. To be inclusive of all possible manifestations of addiction, I have chosen to use the word recovery. I ask you to identify those behaviors that represent relapse, as well as recovery, for yourself.

Each section offers additional tools for your recovery. Knowledge about addiction and recovery is a tool in itself. To remind you of this, at the close of each section there is a toolbox icon. The more tools you gather and use, the stronger your recovery will be. A powerful recovery tool is to acknowledge why you are grateful for each day, so each section concludes with an opportunity to identify what you are grateful for, as well as to reflect on the exercises you have completed. In recovery, we often talk about the need to live "one day at a time."

Recovery is a gift—that is why it is called the present. It is my hope that the moment for reflection will be something you include in your daily practice.

You will see I have a bias toward twelve-step recovery. No other singular resource has been so instrumental in helping great numbers of people recover from addiction in all its forms. If you choose not to utilize twelve-step programs, you will still find this book helpful. I strongly encourage you to take a look at your resistance and try to be more open or actively seek another avenue to support you in recovery. I know of no other life-threatening illness that is as treatable as addiction. At the back of the book you will find contact information for many programs and resources.

My hope for all addicted people is that they find recovery. Know I am with you in spirit.

Addiction History

Getting Started: A Look over Your Shoulder

While you may recognize the power addiction has wielded in your life, this awareness needs to stay at the forefront of your consciousness. Addictive thinking can have you "off and running" toward old attitudes and behaviors before you even realize it. "Getting Started" is an exercise that will help you become centered and focused before you dive into other issues.

Answer the following questions as honestly as possible. Remember, there are no right or wrong answers—only your answers.

When did you first start engaging in your addictive behavior(s)?

_____

_____

_____

_____

_____

_____

Describe the history and progression of your addictive behavior up to the present date.

_____

_____

_____

_____

_____

_____

Review your responses to the first two questions and note the negative consequences of your behavior.

_____

_____

_____

_____

If you have difficulty identifying negative consequences, the examples below will help.

Obsessed or fantasized about addictive behavior

Lied, covered up, or minimized behavior

Physical health affected

Social life affected

Involved in accidents or other dangerous situations

Spirituality affected

Felt guilty or shameful about behaviors

Broke promises to self or others

Denial/minimization of a problem

Primary relationship affected

Financial status affected

Tried to control addictive behavior

Tried to rationalize behavior

Emotional health affected

Parenting skills affected

Had contact with police or courts

Involved in other destructive behavior related to self or others

Experienced depression

Negative feelings about self

Gave up hobbies and interests

Work or school life affected

Manipulated people and situations to support addiction

Powerlessness and Unmanageability

Powerlessness means being unable to stop your addictive behavior(s) despite obvious negative consequences. List examples that demonstrate your powerlessness to stop your addictive behaviors on your own. Be specific about types of behaviors and their frequencies. Start with your earlier examples and conclude with your most recent.

Examples:

      Continued to use despite partner leaving

      Continued to drive despite having a suspended license for DUI

      Continued to see partner in spite of physical abuse

      Continued to purge in spite of related dental problems

1) _____

2) _____

3) _____

4) _____

5) _____

6) _____

7) _____

8) _____

9) _____

10) _____

11) _____

12) _____

13) _____

14) _____

15) _____

Unmanageability means your addiction has created chaos and damage in your life. List as many examples as you can think of that show how your life has become unmanageable as a result of addiction.

Examples:

       Six months ago I was caught stealing to support my habit.

       I had to declare bankruptcy because I maxed out my credit cards buying drugs.

       My wife left me because I had multiple affairs.

       I lost my job for calling in sick too many times.

       I put God out of my life.

       My husband took the kids because I put them in dangerous situations.

1) _____

2) _____

3) _____

4) _____

5) _____

6) _____

7) _____

8) _____

9) _____

10) _____

11) _____

12) _____

13) _____

14) _____

15) _____

Do you have a desire to stop engaging in your addictive behavior(s)?

Yes ☐   No ☐

If yes, list the specific benefits to recovery.

1) _____

2) _____

3) _____

4) _____

5) _____

6) _____

7) _____

8) _____

What difficulties do you anticipate in recovery?

1) _____

2) _____

3) _____

4) _____

5) _____

How would life look in recovery?

_____

_____

_____

_____

Recognize powerlessness

Recognize the unmanageability of addiction

Be aware of being an addict

Identify hope

Today, I am grateful for _____

Overconfidence

Hey, No Problem

Overconfidence is a major threat to recovery. Addicts believe they can handle situations without respect for the dangers of active addiction. Signs of overconfidence include:

- Calling your own shots
- Inability to hear what others are saying
- Feeling contempt prior to investigation
- Wanting immediate results and having unrealistic expectations

Calling your own shots is a first sign of overconfidence. When you first enter into recovery, you may have attended numerous meetings, established a relationship with a sponsor, and started to build a support system.

As time in recovery progresses, people often begin to feel better about themselves and their life in recovery. Once you feel better, it becomes easy to reject what others are suggesting. You begin to replay those old internal tapes. *I know what's best for me* or *I can do it by myself, I have for all these years and I am still alive.* In twelve-step meetings this is known as "yes, butting"—"Yes, but I am not like those people." "Yes, but I am not dead." "Yes, but I have not lost my wife." "Yes, but I have not lost my job."

In essence, you are ready to take back total control of your life. This demonstrates the power of the addictive process and the grandiose thinking that addicts regularly engage in. To paraphrase an Alcoholics Anonymous saying "my best thinking kept me drinking, drugging, gambling, etc." Many people forget what they learned from the First Step of any twelve-step recovery program: they are powerless over their addiction and their lives have become unmanageable.

Inability to hear what others are saying is the second sign of overconfidence. Has this happened to you? You were in a self-help group meeting and discounted what others were saying because you figured it did not apply to you. Addicts are so well practiced at listening to their own voice of denial and justification that they have great difficulty absorbing input from outside sources. Again, they often think, *My situation is different.* "I was sober for about two years," Francine shared. "Then, my old friends invited me to a birthday party. I called my sponsor who told me to avoid the party. I went anyway because I had confidence in myself. When I got there, everybody was using. Before long, I found myself thinking that maybe this time would be different. That was when I relapsed."

Feeling contempt prior to investigation is the third sign of overconfidence. This is a way of discounting methods of recovery that have a long history of proving effective because you don't like them or assume they cannot work for you. Has this happened to you? For example, it was suggested that you go to a Narcotics Anonymous, Alcoholics Anonymous, or another type of twelve-step meeting. After the first fifteen minutes of the meeting, you decide this meeting is not for you. No one there had anything to offer you. Or, perhaps you didn't even bother to try the meeting out. You rejected the idea without any investigation. "I wasn't like those people around me. I hadn't lost everything to my addiction, ended up divorced, lost my house, or anything like that. I left twelve-step meetings because I couldn't identify with how sick those people were."

Wanting immediate results and having unrealistic expectations is the fourth sign of overconfidence. Addicts tend to want immediate results. This is especially true for the addict whose pattern has been one of instant gratification.

You may have said to yourself, "After all, I have been sober six months and my employer still hasn't given me back all of the responsibility I once had."

"My wife does not fully trust me around other women even though I was only unfaithful when I was using. I only used for the last fourteen years."

"I haven't been below my required calorie limit for three weeks now; the doctor isn't being fair about saying it's dangerous to participate in my sport."

The thinking here is *I expect that because I have been in recovery, the world should give me what I want and should give it to me right now. If it doesn't, then why should I put all of this effort into my abstinence?* There is an attitude that the rest of the world owes you. You may think *I've got something coming. I should be rewarded because I have given up so much—my alcohol, drugs, sex, gambling, or other addiction.*

This thinking is often referred to as "terminal uniqueness." It is the belief that your situation is different from everyone else's and that you deserve preferential treatment.

For most people, life in recovery does get better, but it takes time and it is not always in the time frame you prefer. Recovery is a process, not an event. Recovery includes the ability to recognize that others have something of value to offer, and that no one has all the answers.

Remember, it's your best thinking that got you where you were—deep in active addiction.

Rating Signs of Overconfidence

On a scale from 1 to 10, rate how much you identify with each specific form of overconfidence by writing the number of your rating on the lines below. A rating of 1 means you identify with it very little, and a rating of 10 means that you identify with it completely.

Calling your own shots

1 _____ 10

Inability to hear what others are saying

1 _____ 10

Feeling contempt prior to investigation

1 _____ 10

Wanting immediate results and having unrealistic expectations

1 _____ 10

What did you learn?

_____

_____

_____

_____

Are you talking about your overconfidence in your home group? With a sponsor? With a counselor? The first step is recognizing how signs of overconfidence are problematic; the next step is holding those signs up for the light to shine through by talking about it with others.

The following exercises will help you to explore signs of overconfidence more thoroughly.

Calling Your Own Shots

Examples

My wife suggests I not attend a bachelor party, but I went anyway.	Everybody was using; I found myself craving the drug.
I took on an unnecessary additional project at work when I was already stressed even though my sponsor had discouraged it.	I found myself making excuses to not attend recovery meetings.

Identify examples of calling your own shots	Identify the negative consequences you experienced
1)	1)
2)	2)
3)	3)
4)	4)
5)	5)

Inability to Hear What Others Are Saying

Examples

I was told not to drink alcohol, but because my problem was cocaine, I thought that was ridiculous.	Started drinking beer nightly. Within two weeks I was using cocaine.
It was suggested that I not go into convenience stores as they could trigger urges to smoke and gamble.	Within four weeks I was rationalizing I could play the Lotto safely. Within eight weeks I was smoking again and my gambling was out of control.

Identify examples of inability to hear what others are saying	Identify the negative consequences you experienced
1)	1)
2)	2)
3)	3)
4)	4)
5)	5)

Feeling Contempt Prior to Investigation

Examples

I decided the female counselor I was supposed to see wouldn't understand me, so I didn't show up for the session. I don't know if she would have helped me or not.	Quickly returned to negative thinking and sought out previous friends to support it.
I refuse to try meditation because it seems too weird.	I can't find the serenity others seem to find. I continue to feel anxious and stressed.

Identify examples of contempt prior to investigation	Identify the negative consequences
1)	1)
2)	2)
3)	3)
4)	4)
5)	5)

Wanting Immediate Results and Having Unrealistic Expectations

Examples

I expected my children to be loving and fully supportive because I went to treatment.	Became angry with them when I didn't get the loving attitude I expected, and that became a justification for my relapse.
I wanted a job at the same salary level as others at my level of experience.	I refused lower paying jobs, didn't get work, couldn't pay any bills, became resentful, and started acting out.

Identify examples of wanting immediate results and having unrealistic expectations	Identify the negative consequences you experienced
1)	1)
2)	2)
3)	3)
4)	4)
5)	5)

Are you willing to address these issues openly?

Yes ☐   No ☐

If yes, with whom and when will you discuss this?

_____

_____

_____

_____

_____

If no, what are your reasons and concerns?

_____

_____

_____

_____

_____

Be patient

Have an open mind

Listen and hear

Have realistic expectations

Today, I am grateful for _____

Control

I've Got It

An addict went to the horse races and bet everything he had on a particular horse. The bell rings. As the race begins, he looks up into the sky and prays, "God, I really need you today. Please let me win this race and I promise I will never, ever, use drugs again." His horse rounds the first curve and is second to last. As the race goes into the backstretch, his horse is not gaining ground. The addict looks to the sky and says, "God, where are you? I really need you! Please let me win and I promise I will go to a meeting every night." As his horse hits the ¾ pole, it is still trailing. "God, God, I will do service work the rest of my life." Suddenly the horse begins to move up, overtaking one horse after another. Within the last 100 feet, miraculously it pulls into the lead. The addict looks to the sky and says, "That's okay God, I've got it now!"

Did you find this joke funny? Sad? True?

In essence, many people in early recovery can accept that they can't drink or use other drugs, or engage in my other addictive behaviors successfully. But, they struggle to accept the reality that they don't have control over other people, places, and things. The people, places, and things they often still try to control include their co-workers, spouse, kids, and even traffic. The frustration and anger that results from trying to control many things you simply can't will often quickly lead you back to your original, or to new addictive behaviors.

The need and wish for control leads many in early recovery to believe that they can control their addiction. "I know I can't use cocaine anymore, but I can drink because that was never really a problem." Or, "I can't gamble at the race track, but I can play the lottery." Or, "I know it's not wise for me to go to massage parlors, but watching porn on the internet is no big deal." These kinds of beliefs invariably lead to relapse—sometimes later, but frequently sooner.

In what areas of your life are you having difficulty because you are trying to control that which you do not have the power to control?

_____

_____

_____

How would those who know you well answer that question for you?

_____

_____

_____

Giving Up Control

Letting go of control is often extremely difficult to do. However, in order to embrace recovery, you need to surrender to the fact that you are powerless over people, places, and situations. You may be anxious or fearful about what might happen if you give up trying to control people, places, and situations. These emotional reactions are normal and natural.

This exercise is designed to help you identify what letting go of trying to control people, places, and situations would mean in your life. Complete the following sentence stems.

Giving up control in my life would mean:

1) _____

2) _____

3) _____

4) _____

5) _____

When I think about giving up control, I fear:

1) _____

2) _____

3) _____

4) _____

5) _____

Control is often perceived as an all-or-nothing issue. Many of us have fears resulting from ideas about what it means to give up control. Some examples are:

    I will be angry, become violent, hostile, or mean.

    I feel I may physically hurt someone.

    I will lose friendships and offend others.

    My partner will leave.

I won't be heard.
I won't be a real man.
I won't be a real woman.
I will start to cry and not be able to stop.

Look at what you wrote regarding losing control. Where do those thoughts and feelings come from? How old are these thoughts and feelings? How likely is it that those fears will be realized? So often our fears are greater than the reality.

List the negative consequences of your controlling behavior.

1) _____

2) _____

3) _____

4) _____

5) _____

Learning to let go of control takes time. It is not an all-or-nothing proposition. People with addiction often think in black or white, with nothing in-between. In recovery, when we talk about letting go of control, we mean letting go of some control. Learning to not think in terms of all-or-nothing takes time and practice. Recovery takes time. It is a lifelong process that takes place one day at a time.

On the next page is the Serenity Prayer. It reminds us that we don't have control over certain things in our lives, and that there are some things we can change. By saying the Serenity Prayer, we are asking for wisdom and guidance from our Higher Power to helping us distinguish between these two.

The Serenity Prayer

God, grant me the serenity to accept the things I cannot change,
Courage to change the things I can,
And wisdom to know the difference

The Serenity Prayer does not suggest that you give up all control, but to distinguish between what you can change and what you need to accept. Ironically, as you let go of some control, you will actually become more empowered. You will find flexibility where there has only been rigidity. As you let go of control, you can discover greater opportunities to mentally relax, to play, and not carry the burden of the world on your shoulders.

In recovery you have the opportunity to get to know yourself better, to become more honest with yourself and others—to trust, to listen, and to connect. Letting go of control further opens the door to a process of spiritual healing that can come with recovery.

List the positive consequences to letting go of some control.

1) _____

2) _____

3) _____

4) _____

5) _____

Have faith

Live in the process

Today, I am grateful for _____

I'll Handle This

Letting go of self-will means letting go of the need to control, including the need to manipulate people, places, and situations. Controlling behavior is about many things.

- Controlling behavior can be a response to shame. It compensates for the inner belief that says, *I am not adequate; I am insufficient; I am damaged.* You may have carried this message for most of your life.
- Controlling behavior provides a sense of power that helps to compensate for the feelings of shame and not being good enough. It may be a false sense of power, but it is a sense of power nonetheless.
- Growing up in what may have been a dysfunctional home, you may have learned early on in your life that the illusion of having some control in a chaotic environment was critical for survival. Control brings predictability.

However you learned it, there is no need to be critical of your tendency to try to control people and situations. You only need to recognize how it interferes with your recovery today.

There are many styles of control. The four styles listed below are among the most common.

Sweet Controller: Sweet, polite, and pleasant. "And, I always get what I want."

Distant Controller: Emotionally cold, rigidly efficient, and a master of details.

Passive Controller: "I don't care. It doesn't matter to me." But, the reality is that it does matter—a lot. Otherwise known as the Martyr.

Angry Controller: "I want what I want when I want it. And, I will darn well get it." The Intimidator.

What style(s) of control did your parents use?

_____

_____

What style(s) of control do you use today?

_____

_____

_____

Regardless of the style of control, those with a need for control operate from a position of fear, shame, and distrust. There are a variety of negative consequences for controlling behavior. They may not know how to listen or follow direction. They may lack in creativity or spontaneity. They may withhold thoughts and feelings, and intimidate people. For many people the need for control is a major barrier to recovery. Faith and control do not peacefully coexist. If you are searching for intimacy, you won't find it without letting go of control.

Trying to control people and situations requires a tremendous amount of energy, and often leaves controllers frustrated, angry, resentful, or depressed because their efforts to control ultimately fail. In order to let go of attempting to control events and other people in your life, you need to increase your understanding of your responsibility for your feelings and actions.

Letting Go of Self Will

As you answer these questions, rate yourself on a scale of 1 to 10, with 1 meaning the least and 10 the most.

Are you usually unselfish or do you put your needs before the needs of others?

If the latter, give an example.

Unselfish-1 _____ 10-Selfish

_____

If you rated yourself 7 or above or 3 or less, do you think this area contributes to the possibility of relapse for you?

Yes ☐   No ☐

If yes, explain:

_____

_____

_____

Do you usually admit and take responsibility when you are wrong, or do you make excuses, justifications, or blame others? If the latter, give an example.

Responsible-1 _____10-Blame, justify

_____

Do you usually let go and forgive, or do you hold onto resentments and self-pity?

If the latter, give an example.

Forgiveness-1 _____10-Resentment

_____

_____

_____

Do you tend to deal with problems directly, or do you procrastinate or avoid dealing with problems? If the latter, give an example.

Act-1 _____10-Avoid

_____

_____

_____

If you rated yourself 7 or above on any of these scales, do you think this area contributes to the possibility of relapse?

Yes ☐　　　　　　　No ☐

If yes, explain:

_____

_____

_____

If letting go of control is a problematic area for you, identify on a daily basis two areas in which you want to practice "letting go." It may be the same two areas repeatedly, but staying aware of your intention to let go of the need for control will help you to follow through on it.

One way to do this is in the context of a morning meditation. You can use the sentence stem,

"Today I will let go of control of _____."

Remember that each day in recovery, learning to let go of your need to control helps you to stay in the moment; to trust in your Higher Power; to accept that you don't have to have all the answers.

Can identify self-will behaviors

Am accountable

Consider others

Am willing to let go

Identify controlling behaviors

Today, I am grateful for _____

Feelings

Name That Feeling

Relapse Connection

Check in the box that most accurately describes your experience:

☐ I engage in my addictive behavior(s) because I want my feelings to go away

☐ I engage in my addictive behavior(s) because I want to let my feelings out

Are there specific feelings you are trying to avoid or express? If yes, name them.

_____

_____

To many people, addictive disorders represent a world that is quiet and soothing and takes away their pain—at least for a short while.

Alan, a thirty-two-year-old addict, said, "I was eleven when I took my first drink. I hated the taste, but I felt the warm glow and it worked. I would get sick as a dog, but would still do it again. I got drunk because I had a hole in my gut and alcohol filled it up. Alcohol and drugs became the solution. There was one reason I drank and used. It was to get blithering numb. And when I was numb, not a thing or person could hurt me; I felt nothing."

Often, the attraction to addictive behaviors is that they serve to medicate inner pain. For so many in recovery, abstaining from whatever form of addiction addicts were engaged in results in experiencing something they spent years trying to avoid—their feelings. For many people in early recovery, the fear and discomfort of feeling their emotions contributes to relapse.

The inability to express and feel safe with feelings frequently begins with experiences in one's family of origin at an early age. Many addicts grow up in dysfunctional or abusive homes where it was not safe to express feelings. As a result, they live with much fear, disappointment, sadness, and embarrassment. They witnessed intense anger, pain, and rage. It was a very lonely time.

A show of feelings was frequently met with disapproval, rejection, or even punishment. If they showed any feelings at all, they often were rejected. They were given such shaming messages as "Big boys or girls don't cry," "Don't be such a sissy," or "I'll really give you something to cry about." The message, whether delivered overtly or covertly, was clear—it is not okay to be your own person with individual feelings, desires, or needs. Feelings need to be avoided at all costs.

Recovery includes the ability to tolerate feelings without needing to medicate them.

The following questions begin the process of understanding your "feeling" self.

What two feelings are easiest for you to express in front of other people?

1) _____

2) _____

What two feelings are most difficult for you to express in front of other people?

1) _____

2) _____

We often mask painful feelings with forms of self-protection. For example, we may mask sadness with humor, fear with intellectualizing, anger with social isolation. By identifying when you use such defenses, you are a step closer to recognizing the underlying feelings.

Examine one of the difficult feelings you just identified. When you begin to experience this feeling, what do you do to mask or defend against it?

_____

_____

_____

_____

_____

Take a feeling that you mask—one that is difficult for you to show others. Identify the fear(s) that gets in the way of your showing that feeling. Common fears are: Someone will think I'm stupid. People will take advantage of me. I wouldn't be in control. What are your fears?

_____

_____

_____

Most fear comes from your personal history, starting when you were a child. For you, the fear is real, but more often than not, it is based in history rather than present-day realities. If you are frightened of sharing feelings, you need to ask yourself if you are carrying past experiences into the present. Sometimes, addicts have a tremendous amount of unexpected energy surrounding a situation. Should your fears be based in present-day experiences, then discussing them with a safe person will help decrease them. It is only by acknowledging and expressing your fears that you can put them to rest.

Feelings

We have many feelings, some we are willing to expose to others, and others we choose to keep hidden. Identify the feelings you experienced (whether or not you expressed them) in the age ranges indicated below. The following list of feelings is only a partial one; feel free to add your own.

People often have more than one feeling at a time, and those feelings may seem contrary to each other. One can love and hate, be sad and angry, be fearful and happy at the same time. This does not mean you are crazy; it means you have reasons to be fearful and happy, angry and sad, or to hate and love at the same time.

love	anger	bravery	confusion	anxiousness
hurt	gloom	shyness	happiness	embarrassment
fear	guilt	patience	moodiness	disappointment
hate	caring	jealousy	excitement	encouragement
worry	warmth	joy	frustration	discouragement
shame	sadness	resentment	loneliness	

Age	Expressed Feelings	Unexpressed Feelings
Before 12	_____	_____
	_____	_____
	_____	_____
12 to 17	_____	_____
	_____	_____
	_____	_____
18 to 24	_____	_____
	_____	_____
	_____	_____
25 to 34	_____	_____
	_____	_____
	_____	_____
35 to 44	_____	_____
	_____	_____
	_____	_____
45 to 54	_____	_____
	_____	_____
	_____	_____
55 to 64	_____	_____
	_____	_____
	_____	_____

65 + _____ _____

        _____ _____

        _____ _____

What did you learn? _____

_____

_____

Identify feelings

Let go of defenses

Today, I am grateful for _____

The "F" Word: Fear

Many people grow up with chronic fear. Even though fear was frequently experienced, it is often denied. Whether or not these fears are recognized, they are usually carried into adulthood. Addictive substances and behaviors can medicate your fear. But once you are clean and sober, you become more aware of your fear. Sometimes, it is general or "free-floating," rather than connected to something specific. In some instances, it is pervasive and seems ever-present. Fear can also appear episodically, appearing quickly and powerfully, then disappearing almost as suddenly.

Make a list of four situations growing up in which you remember being fearful and note whether or not you expressed that fear.

1) _____

2) _____

3) _____

4) _____

Check the behaviors that describe what you did as a child when you felt afraid:

☐ Acted unafraid

☐ Cried

☐ Got angry

☐ Hid (where?) _____

☐ Told someone about my fear

☐ Other (fill in) _____

When I was afraid, my mom usually

☐ Never noticed

☐ Noticed, but ignored it

☐ Made me feel embarrassed or ashamed

☐ Made me feel better

☐ Other (fill in) _____

When I was afraid, my dad usually

    ☐ Never noticed

    ☐ Noticed, but ignored it

    ☐ Made me feel embarrassed or ashamed

    ☐ Made me feel better

    ☐ Other (fill in) _____

If there was a particular person—a brother, sister, or other significant person in your life—that responded to your fear (either negatively or positively), identify who they were and describe how they responded.

_____

_____

_____

Expressing Fear

To better understand how you experience fear as an adult, complete the following sentences:

When I am afraid, I

_____

_____

_____

_____

When I am afraid, I

_____

_____

_____

_____

If people knew I was afraid,

_____

_____

_____

_____

If people knew I was afraid,

_____

_____

_____

_____

Fear Today

There are many valid reasons to feel fear, but these can be distorted by addictive thinking. You might find the following acronyms relevant: FEAR—False Evidence Appearing Real or Forget Everything And Run. If you identify with either of these, it will be helpful to use them as reminders of how addictive thinking can magnify feelings of fear or create needless fears.

In early recovery, the fears are many and include:
- If people really knew me they would reject me
- I'll never be good enough
- I'm too set in my ways to change
- My life is over

Complete the following exercise. Identify your present day fears. On the right-hand side of the page, list people with whom you have shared that specific fear or are willing to share that fear with now.

Today I feel afraid about: Name

1) _____   _____

_____

_____

2) _____   _____

_____

_____

3) _____   _____

_____

_____

What are the positives of owning fear?

    ☐ Relief

    ☐ Being less controlled

    ☐ Greater physical health

    ☐ Not hiding pain

    ☐ Being more honest

    ☐ Other _____

Identify and own fears

Know self better

Today, I am grateful for _____

How Do You Plead—Guilty?

Guilt is a feeling of regret or remorse about something we have or have not done. While guilt is a healthy emotion that facilitates social conscience, it can be distorted if you were raised in a dysfunctional family. Often when problems occur, family members blame each other—wives blame husbands, husbands blame wives, partners blame partners, parents blame children, children blame parents, children blame each other. Young children, because they are defenseless, most readily accept and internalize the blame, even when they have done nothing to deserve it. This often morphs into feelings of guilt.

You may not be aware that you have internalized guilt as intensely as you have until you see yourself acting it out by repeatedly apologizing when you have done nothing wrong, chronically taking care of others at your expense, or having feelings of depression.

Childhood Guilt

Check the boxes of the family members about whom you felt guilt for things that took place when you were a child.

☐ Mom

_____

_____

☐ Dad

_____

_____

☐ Sister (name)

_____

_____

☐ Brother (name)

_____

_____

☐ Brother (name)

_____

_____

☐ Other (name)

_____

_____

☐ Sister (name) ☐ Other (name)

_____ _____

_____ _____

For each box you checked above, give two reasons that prompted your guilt. For example:

   I felt responsible for Mom and Dad's arguing because they often argued about me.
   I felt responsible for my brother getting hit—I should have been able to stop my dad.
   I felt responsible for not being able to make my mom happier.
   I could have gotten better grades at school.

Check each box that describes how you behaved as a child when you felt guilty:

   ☐ Ate to stuff my feelings of guilt

   ☐ Hid (Where?) _____

   ☐ Apologized

   ☐ Cleaned the house

   ☐ Tried to act "good"

   ☐ Other (fill in) _____

   ☐ Other (fill in) _____

When I felt guilty, my mom usually

   ☐ Never knew

   ☐ Reinforced my guilt by blaming me for things I did not do

   ☐ Made me feel even more guilty

   ☐ Punished me even if I was not at fault

   ☐ Made me feel that I was not responsible, helping to lessen my guilt

   ☐ Other (fill in) _____

When I felt guilty, my dad usually

- ☐ Never knew
- ☐ Reinforced my guilt by blaming me for things I did not do
- ☐ Made me feel even more guilty
- ☐ Punished me even if I was not at fault
- ☐ Made me feel that I was not responsible, helping to lessen my guilt
- ☐ Other (fill in) _____

What do you do when you feel guilty today?

_____

_____

_____

False Guilt

Because children have limited mental, physical, and emotional resources, a major part of parenting involves physically and psychologically protecting their children. Children need security, love, caring, and honesty in order to grow in healthy ways. Unfortunately, many parents are not able to meet these needs on a consistent basis. In some of these families, children attempt to fill the void and assume parental responsibilities. But, these are young children—children who do not yet have the ability to act as responsible adults. Not only do parents often ask children to take responsibility for things that adults are normally responsible for, they often insinuate that their children are the cause of their (the adults') problems. Because of their dependency on their parents, children usually believe that their parents know everything and accept their parents' every word. As a result, young children have a distorted view of their power. They come to believe they have power to affect people, places, and situations far more than they truly can. This contributes to a false sense of guilt and an overwhelming sense of powerlessness.

Do you have a history of taking on false guilt?

Yes ☐   No ☐

Do you take on false guilt today?

Yes ☐   No ☐

If you answered yes, complete the following exercise.

Saying No to False Guilt

We often have a distorted perception of where our power lies and, as a result, live with false guilt. While true guilt is remorse or regret we feel for something we have or have not done, false guilt is taking on the feeling of guilt related to someone else's actions. It is important to gain a realistic perspective of situations that we have the power to affect.

Because this is usually a lifelong habit, it is important to go back and delineate historically what you were and were not responsible for. That will help you become more skilled in recognizing your patterns of assuming false guilt, and discontinuing it.

Reflect back on your childhood and adolescence, consider the things you feel guilty about and say no to each situation. Say, "No! I wasn't responsible for _____." "No! It wasn't my fault; it wasn't my obligation."

Write "No!" in each blank and then continue by finishing the sentence:

_____, I was not responsible for _____

when he/she _____

_____, I was not responsible for _____

when he/she _____

_____, it wasn't my fault when _____

_____, it wasn't my fault when _____

_____, it wasn't my duty or obligation to _____

_____, it wasn't my duty or obligation to _____

_____, it wasn't my duty or obligation to _____

_____, it wasn't my duty or obligation to _____

What do you feel false guilt about today?

1) _____

2) _____

3) _____

4) _____

5) _____

Guilt Today

List the people and situations about which you feel guilt today.

Today I feel guilt about:

1) _____

_____

_____

2) _____

_____

_____

3) _____

_____

_____

While it is common to be confused about false guilt, the reality is that addicts (regardless of the forms of addiction) are responsible for their own behavior. In your addiction you have hurt other people.

- Cindy, a codependent, is guilty for not attending to her children's needs appropriately because she is caught up in her addiction to relationships. She is preoccupied with where and when her next relationship will be occurring.
- Bill, an alcoholic, is guilty for continuing to lie to his partner and friends.
- Jake, a compulsive overeater, is guilty for his lying.
- Jessica is guilty for her stealing to support her gambling.

Step Eight of the Twelve Steps states, "We made a list of all persons we had harmed, and became willing to make amends to them all." Step Nine states, "We made direct amends to such people whenever possible, except when to do so would injure them or others."

Have you completed Steps Eight and Nine in a twelve-step program?

Yes ☐   No ☐

If yes, describe your experience working these steps?

_____

_____

_____

If you have completed these steps, is it possible you omitted certain people?

Yes ☐   No ☐

If you haven't done these steps, what has gotten in the way of doing them?

_____

_____

_____

Do you have a home group?

Yes ☐   No ☐

Do you have a sponsor?

      Yes ☐   No ☐

There is an appropriate time and a place for making amends. Amends are much more than just verbal apologies. In addition to words, they take the form of healthy behaviors. For example, if you are feeling guilty about not previously showing up at your daughter's ballgame, you can show up at her ballgame today and at her games in the future. If you are guilty for stealing from a relative's home, you can begin to make payments. If you are guilty for raging at family members, you can enroll in an anger management course and change your behavior.

Identify three behaviors that would be part of your amends to others right now.

1) _____

2) _____

3) _____

What are the positives of owning guilt?

      ☐ Relief

      ☐ Being less controlled

      ☐ Greater physical health

      ☐ Not hiding pain

      ☐ Being more honest

      ☐ Other _____

Identify and own guilt

Know self better

Distinguish true from false guilt

Today, I am grateful for _____

Cry Me a River—or a Drought

With loss there is sadness, and with sadness often there are tears. Feeling sad and crying are a natural part of being human. If you did not receive validation for your sadness growing up—if you experienced negative responses when you expressed sadness—you probably began to control how you expressed that emotion. As is the case with most other emotions, the way you express your sadness has likely been scripted since childhood. You may find yourself without the ability to cry. Or, you may find that after years of seldom crying, you cry frequently and are unable to identify the reasons for your tears.

The next few exercises are designed to help you identify sadness and better understand how you perceive crying.

Past Sadness

In some families, certain things that were said or occurred caused sadness. In others, sadness was caused by what wasn't said or didn't occur. Sadness from childhood can be related to many experiences, including moving multiple times and having to change friends, parents failing to attend school or sports events, or never being told that you were loved.

Complete the following sentence.

When I was a child or teenager, I can remember feeling sad about (whether or not anyone else knew that you were sad):

1) _____

2) _____

3) _____

Check the behaviors that describe what you did as a child when you felt sad.

- ☐ Cried when I was alone
- ☐ Cried in front of others
- ☐ Went to bed
- ☐ Took a walk

☐ Told someone about my sadness

☐ Other (fill in) _____

☐ Other (fill in) _____

When I felt sad, my mom usually

☐ Never noticed

☐ Noticed, but ignored it

☐ Made me feel embarrassed or ashamed

☐ Made me feel better

☐ Other (fill in) _____

When I felt sad, my dad usually

☐ Never noticed

☐ Noticed, but ignored it

☐ Made me feel embarrassed or ashamed

☐ Made me feel better

☐ Other (fill in) _____

If there was particular people—a brother, sister, or other significant person in your life—who responded to your sadness (either negatively or positively), identify who they were and describe how they responded.

_____

_____

_____

Expressing Sadness without Tears

This exercise is to help you identify whether you have difficulty expressing sadness with tears and whether you have fears about crying.

Complete the following sentences.

When I cry, I

_____

_____

_____

When I cry, I feel

_____

_____

_____

If people see me cry, I

_____

_____

_____

If you were unable to complete the previous exercise because you never cry, complete the following statements.

I never cry because

_____

_____

_____

If I ever did cry, I would

_____

_____

_____

I might have felt better if I'd cried when

_____

_____

_____

Sadness Today

Addiction creates loss. Where there is loss there is sadness. You may be sad about distant relationships with your children, for the pain addiction has caused in your most intimate relationships, for how you have hurt friends, and/or because a major part of your life is irretrievable.

Complete the following exercise. Identify your present-day sadness. On the right hand side of the page, list people with whom you have shared each specific episode of sadness or are willing to share that sadness with now.

Today I feel sad about: Name

1) _____   _____

_____   _____

_____   _____

2) _____   _____

_____   _____

_____   _____

3) _____   _____

  _____   _____

  _____   _____

What are the positives of owning sadness?

☐ Relief

☐ Being less controlled

☐ Greater physical health

☐ Not hiding pain

☐ Being more honest

☐ Other _____

Identify and own fears

Know self better

Identify and own sadness

Today, I am grateful for _____

Angry? Me?

For many addicts, anger avoidance is a key issue. You have learned from an early age to quickly diffuse your anger to avoid negative consequences. You have internalized this model and as an adult avoid anger to keep yourself safe. You avoid anger because anger may have a variety of emotional issues attached to it. You may have had a parent who was consistently forceful with their anger and now want to avoid expressing your own anger so as not to be like your parent.

You may have a variety of personal beliefs that preclude you from expressing anger.

    Healthy people don't get angry

    I will be shamed and blamed by others

    Being angry means losing control

Expressing Anger

Many times people have little awareness of their anger. You may be frightened of your anger, or frightened of other people's anger, or you may have so much anger that you feel as though you might explode. If you have difficulty expressing anger, it is important to explore how you perceive this powerful emotion.

Complete the following sentences.

When I am angry, I

_____

_____

_____

When I am angry, I feel

_____

_____

_____

If people see me angry, I feel

_____

_____

_____

When people get angry, I

_____

_____

_____

If you were unable to complete the previous exercise because you are never angry, complete the following statements.

I'm never angry because

_____

_____

_____

If I ever got angry, I'd

_____

_____

_____

I might have felt better if I'd gotten angry when

_____

_____

_____

Complete the following sentence.

When I was a child or teenager, I can remember being angry about . . . (whether or not anyone else knew that you were angry):

1) _____

2) _____

3) _____

If you have difficulty identifying your anger, you may want to think in terms of feeling "frustrated," "disgusted," "irritated," or "upset about." If that helps, go back to the previous exercise and try it again using these alternative terms.

Potential Anger

If you still have difficulty identifying your anger, try thinking of five things that took place in your childhood and adolescence that you could have been angry about. You may not have felt angry, but the situation was frustrating and the potential for anger was there. Another way of looking at it is to imagine a young child at age five, seven, nine, etc., and put him/her in your family in the same situation. Make a list of what this child could be angry about.

1) _____

2) _____

3) _____

4) _____

5) _____

Check the behaviors that describe what you did as a child when you were angry.

☐ Pouted

☐ Screamed (at whom?)

☐ Was sarcastic

☐ Told the person with whom I was angry directly about my anger

☐ Hit harder on the ball field (or other sport)

☐ Ate to stuff my anger

☐ Ran away

☐ Other (fill in) _____

☐ Other (fill in) _____

When I was angry, my mom usually

☐ Never noticed

☐ Noticed, but ignored it

☐ Made me feel embarrassed or ashamed

☐ Made me feel better

☐ Other (fill in) _____

When I was angry, my dad usually

☐ Never noticed

☐ Noticed, but ignored it

☐ Made me feel embarrassed or ashamed

☐ Made me feel better

☐ Other (fill in) _____

If there was another person—brother, sister, or someone else significant in your life—who responded to your anger (either negatively or positively), identify who they were and describe how they responded.

_____

_____

_____

Anger Today

Identify your present-day anger, and list the people with whom you have shared that specific anger with or whom you are willing to share that anger with now.

Today I feel angry about: Name

1) _____   _____

_____   _____

_____   _____

2) _____   _____

_____   _____

_____   _____

3) _____   _____

_____   _____

_____   _____

What are the positives of owning and letting yourself feel your anger?

☐ Relief

☐ Being less controlled

☐ Greater physical health

☐ Not hiding pain

☐ Being more honest

☐ Other _____

Identify fear

Identify and own anger

Know self better

Today, I am grateful for _____

Anger

Aristotle's Challenge

Anyone can become angry . . . that is easy. But to be angry
with the right person, to the right degree, at the right time for
the purpose, and in the right way, that is not so easy.
—Aristotle

When angry, count to ten before speaking out; if
very angry, count to one hundred.
—Thomas Jefferson

Check the statement that best describes the relationship between your anger and your addictive behavior.

☐ I act out (use) because I want to let my anger out

☐ I act out (use) because I want my anger to go away

☐ I act out (use) to get back at others

☐ I act out (use) when I get so frustrated I'm not willing to care about anything

☐ I act out (use) to hurt or punish myself

A Hole in the Sidewalk

Describe in more detail how your anger and your addictive behavior are related.

_____

_____

_____

_____

Unhealthy anger can present itself in a variety of ways.

1) Anger can be overtly expressed with yelling or shaming statements, "You are so stupid, you can't get anything right!"

2) Anger can be covertly expressed. Anger expressed covertly often is passive-aggressive, and may involve procrastinating, being late, using sarcasm, or making demeaning comments toward others. Family members with unresolved issues between one another may make fun of the other family member. While the content may be delivered in a joking manner, underneath the surface is anger. This is sometimes referred to as guerrilla humor. You make a hostile remark to somebody with a smile. Should they call you on it, you tell them it was a joke, and often insult them again, by asking them why don't they have a "sense of humor."

3) Anger can be retaliatory. This occurs when you find a way to settle a score. Addicts often keep a mental log of who has wronged them and seek ways to get even.

4) Anger can be masked as isolation. *I don't like people, they don't like me, and that is just fine. I don't need people. I don't need anything from anybody, ever.*

5) Anger can be manifested as depression. Unresolved grief, pain, shame, and trauma, can result in tremendous anger—which turned inward often becomes depression. In some contexts, it can be safer and more socially acceptable to be depressed rather than angry.

6) Anger, which is a feeling, can move into rage, which is a behavior.

With rage there is no middle ground. It is as if rageful people are walking around with a match in one hand and a gas can in the other. All someone has to do is give those who turn their anger into rage the wrong look or not respond as quickly as they would like and suddenly they are yelling, blaming, accusing, and maybe physically hitting someone. They can move from the temperature of ten degrees to one hundred degrees within seconds.

Check the following ways of expressing anger with which you identify.

☐ Yelling

☐ Shaming statements

☐ Being sarcastic

☐ Guerrilla humor

☐ Being late

☐ Wanting or needing to "settle the score"

☐ Avoiding anger

☐ Isolation

☐ Depression

☐ Raging behavior(s)

Anger clouds judgment; harms relationships, and can lead to violence, as well as to relapse.

Identify how you have been hurtful to others in expressing your anger.

Example: It was (is) hurtful to (person's name) when I _____

It was (is) hurtful to _____ when I _____

It was (is) hurtful to _____ when I _____

It was (is) hurtful to _____ when I _____

It was (is) hurtful to _____ when I _____

It was (is) hurtful to _____ when I _____

It was (is) hurtful to _____ when I _____

It was (is) hurtful to _____ when I _____

It was (is) hurtful to _____ when I _____

Identify how you have been hurtful to yourself in expressing your anger?

I hurt myself by _____

I hurt myself by _____

I hurt myself by _____

I hurt myself by _____

I hurt myself by _____

I hurt myself by _____

I hurt myself by _____

I hurt myself by _____

Anger Sentence Stems

Your formative years strongly influenced the way you express your feelings today. The following exercise may offer you some valuable insight. Think back on when you were growing up and complete the following sentences.

When my dad got angry, he _____

When my dad got angry, he _____

When my dad got angry, I _____

When my dad got angry, I _____

When my mom got angry, she _____

When my mom got angry, she _____

When my mom got angry, I _____

When my mom got angry, I _____

When I got angry at my mom, she _____

When I got angry at my mom, she _____

When I got angry at my dad, he _____

When I got angry at my dad, he _____

Today when I get angry, I _____

Today when I get angry, I _____

There is a huge difference between learning about your anger and learning how to not act on it in ways that are hurtful. These exercises are meant to help you recognize the significance of anger in your life and your recovery. The more significant anger has been in your life, the more important it is to pay attention to it and work on it in your recovery. I encourage you to seek feedback in your recovery group and, as needed, with a counselor/therapist.

Identify how anger relates to use of addictive substances or processes

Identify personal anger expressions

Own negative consequences of anger

Recognize family anger patterns

Today, I am grateful for _____

Mad . . . and It's Not about You

It is not uncommon for people to use their anger as an excuse to engage in their addiction.

Tim comes home from work agitated and anxious, but he isn't sure why. He has not gambled in four weeks, deliberately staying away from his gambling sites—the horse races and sports bars. He has been feeling depressed, has withdrawn socially, and is not sharing his concerns or fears.

As he walks through the door, his teenage daughter races out, telling him she is going out with her boyfriend and will be back late. Tim hates her boyfriend. He rummages through the kitchen, hungry, wondering why his wife and other daughter are not home. He notices the blinking light on the answering machine, listens to the message that his wife is at her sister's for the weekend and his other daughter is spending the night with a friend.

That does it! He doesn't need her and his kids obviously don't need him. So why is he depriving himself? He grabs the car keys, slams the door as he leaves the house, and peels rubber as he drives to the local sports bar.

Tim may have legitimate reasons to be frustrated about his relationship with his wife and daughters, but he used his righteous sense of anger as an excuse to return to gambling.

Identify situations in your life when you used anger as a vehicle to justify resuming your addictive behavior.

1) _____

2) _____

3) _____

4) _____

Recognize how anger can fuel addiction

Today, I am grateful for _____

Hostility Roadmap

Identify the last three situations that made you angry.

1) _____

_____

_____

2) _____

_____

_____

3) _____

_____

_____

How did you respond in these situations?

1) _____

_____

_____

2) _____

_____

_____

3) _____

_____

_____

Look at the **Hostility Road Map** to see how to effectively respond.

HOSTILITY ROADMAP WITH STRATEGIES
Cynical Thought . . . Angry Feeling . . . Aggressive Action

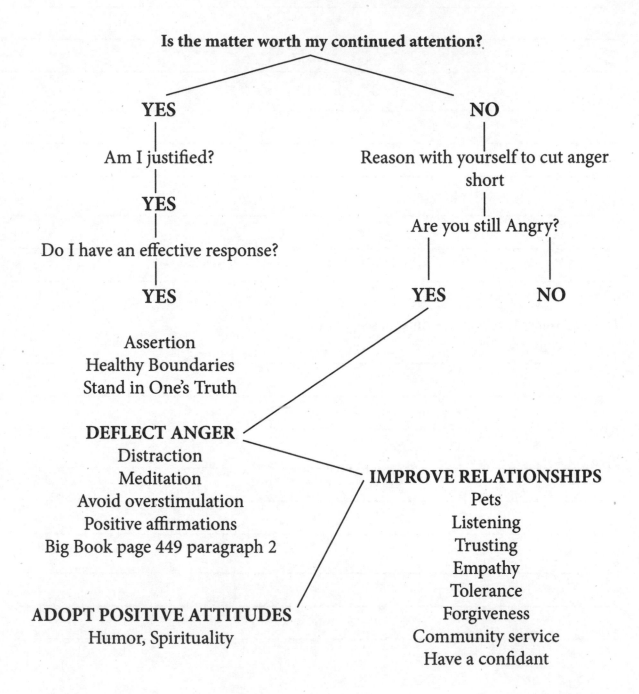

Is the matter worth my continued attention?

YES   **NO**

Am I justified?   Reason with yourself to cut anger short

YES

Do I have an effective response?   Are you still Angry?

YES   **YES**   **NO**

Assertion
Healthy Boundaries
Stand in One's Truth

DEFLECT ANGER
Distraction
Meditation
Avoid overstimulation
Positive affirmations
Big Book page 449 paragraph 2

IMPROVE RELATIONSHIPS
Pets
Listening
Trusting
Empathy
Tolerance
Forgiveness
Community service
Have a confidant

ADOPT POSITIVE ATTITUDES
Humor, Spirituality

Following are examples of situations that might anger you and cause you to respond in a hostile manner. Using the tools provided in the Hostility Roadmap, see how effective responses were developed.

Example:

Another driver cuts me off on my way to work and I am infuriated.

Is the matter worth my continued attention? No.

Reason with yourself to diffuse your anger. *He didn't see me. I am nervous about my meeting today at work and I am overreacting.*

Example:

I am angry at my seventeen-year-old for wrecking my car.

Am I justified? Yes.

Do I have an effective response? No. I want to say, "You stupid so and so, I can't trust you with anything."

Reason with yourself to your diffuse you anger. *I wrecked my dad's car when I was fourteen. He didn't take time to even drive with me and I thought it was funny. Maybe I need to take more time with my son in the car, for the sake of spending time, not just driving.*

Are you still angry? No, not so much.

Now look at the three situations that made you angry and develop your own Roadmap for your responses.

Situation 1

_____

_____

_____

Situation 2

_____

_____

_____

Situation 3

_____

_____

_____

Evaluate justification for anger

Identify effective responses

Today, I am grateful for _____

Resentments

Whose Poison Is It?

Resentments are like burrs in a saddle blanket: if you do not get rid of them, they fester into an infection. James, who is nine months sober, is working in a real estate office for an employer who is twelve years sober. James relapses and enters treatment. When he returns to work, he feels misunderstood because he was not welcomed back with open arms. In his hurt and confusion, he becomes angry and resentful. He finds another job and stops attending twelve-step meetings. If he sees his former boss, he makes an effort to avoid him. When asked why he is so resentful, all he can say is that his former boss is a jerk.

Karen, new to recovery for her anorexia, is resentful toward her sister whom she believes is also anorexic and not seeking recovery.

Tim, a sex addict, is immediately resentful when his wife rejects his sexual advances and uses his resentment to fuel acting out.

Resentment is a common emotional reaction to the experience of feeling discounted, slighted, wronged, or unheard. Many times the person you are feeling slighted by is totally unaware of the behavior you interpreted as a personal harm or insult.

There is a twelve-step saying that holding on to resentments is the equivalent of swallowing poison and the hoping the person whom you are resentful toward will die. A Buddhist perspective describes anger as an acid that eats away at the vessel holding it.

Part of the foundation of all twelve-step programs is that when someone or something bothers you, it has more to do with what goes on inside of you than with the other person or situation. What happens to you is less important than what you do with what happens to you. Learning how to accept things as they are, instead of fighting against them is what makes peace of mind and serenity possible.

How does hanging on to resentments affect you?

_____

_____

_____

What would it mean to accept that you have been hurt or wronged and you cannot change that reality?

_____

_____

_____

What does it mean to take responsibility for your own feelings?

_____

_____

_____

Ultimately, who pays the price for hanging on to resentments?

_____

_____

_____

Today, are you willing to let go of your resentments?

      Yes ☐   No ☐

If no, what do you get from you holding onto them?

_____

_____

_____

_____

In order to maintain their resentments, people often seek out others who will support their indignant feelings of having been wronged. After all, misery enjoys company. Unfortunately, most of the time people willing to support resentments are not in recovery. As a result, if you're looking for support for your resentments, you may gravitate toward using friends who are most apt to support your negativity.

Resentments are often built on assumptions. "When you don't look at me, I assume that you are disrespecting me, or that you think you are better than me." "When you don't include me in a social gathering, I assume that you think that I am not good enough to be your friend."

Resentments are built on entitlement—a form of unrealistic expectations combined with impatience. "I have been in recovery for six weeks. My wife should trust me by now." "Because I am changing, I should be rewarded." "Now that I am in recovery, my boss should give me that promotion I deserve." "I am owed _____. I deserve _____."

An equation that may be helpful to remember is: unrealistic expectations + impatience = resentments.

The following exercise will help you identify how resentments may be present in your life.

Examples might be:
 I resent that I am an addict.
 I resent that in recovery I can't live like I used to.
 I resent the guy who sits next to me in meetings. He just looks like he thinks he is
 better than me.
 I resent all the amends I need to make for my past behaviors.

I am resentful that _____

I am resentful that _____

I am resentful that _____

I am resentful that _____

I am resentful that _____

One of the ways to move away from resentment is to ask yourself, what is this resentment potentially covering up? Are resentment and anger covering up another feeling? An example of this is resenting the amends process in which addicts need to engage. You may be filled with guilt about your past behavior and anxious and fearful of the other person's feelings and reactions to the amends process.

This resentment could be reframed as, *I am afraid of my feelings when making amends to others. I feel guilty and I am scared.*

Resentments are also about control. Resenting others is often about resenting those who have interfered or you believe will interfere with your plans. If this could be true for you, refer back to section on Control.

Different ways to move away from a place of resentment are:
- When assuming, check it out.
- Put yourself in somebody else's shoes—it may allow expectations to be more realistic.
- Identify and own the feelings the resentment is covering up.
- Be willing to live and let live.

From the resentments you listed, explore ways to move away from that place of resentment.

My resentment is:

_____

_____

_____

Different ways I can move from my place of resentment are:

_____

_____

_____

My resentment is:

_____

_____

_____

Different ways I can move from my place of resentment are:

_____

_____

_____

My resentment is:

_____

_____

_____

Different ways I can move from my place of resentment are:

_____

_____

_____

Twelve-step work is vital to addressing and working through resentments. Specifically, Steps Four, Five, Eight, and Nine are related to resentments and amends.

Have you done Steps Four, Five, Eight, and Nine?

Yes ☐   No ☐

If so, how was your experience working these Steps?

_____

_____

_____

This is a good time to review them and see if you have left anything out.

If you haven't done these Steps, what has gotten in the way of doing them?

_____

_____

_____

Do you have a home group?

     Yes ☐   No ☐

Do you have a sponsor?

     Yes ☐   No ☐

When you hold on to resentments, your focus is externally directed. This takes valuable time and energy away from looking at your own issues—your thoughts, feelings, and behaviors—including how you may have contributed to the situation about which you are resentful. They can only obstruct your progress in recovery. As long as your attention is directed toward others and what they have done to you, it is difficult, if not impossible, to pay attention to what you can do to take better care of your thoughts and feelings, and use this self-care to guide your behavior in ways that will support your recovery.

It is important to be aware when you are experiencing and holding on to resentments, and to move toward addressing them constructively.

Understand danger of resentments

Identify resentments

Identify ways to let go of resentments

Today, I am grateful for _____

The Needle Is In the Red Zone

As described in the last section, learning about your resentments is an essential part of a program of recovery. In order to learn how to release resentments, you need to know the specific themes of your resentments and how they show up in your life.

Having listed specific resentments in a previous exercise, can you identify any particular themes in your resentments? Do they tend to relate to specific people (or types of people) or issues?

_____

_____

_____

Resentments often stem from unrealistic expectations or distorted thinking. When people in recovery are resentful, they often lose their serenity and in acting out of anger experience a SLIP—Sobriety Losing Its Priority.

The following exercise is designed to help you identify resentments, the thinking associated with resentments, and the consequences. Example:

I am resentful at	For	What I told myself that was unrealistic or distorted	What I did
My co-worker	Not including me in a project	He didn't value my work; I'm not good enough	I got loaded
My spouse	Having friends	I should have all of my wife's attention whenever I want it	I had affairs
My sponsor	Spending time with others	He wasn't available when I wanted him to be	I didn't follow directions

I am resentful at	For	What I told myself that was unrealistic or distorted	What I did

Looking back at the resentments you listed, what role did you have in the situation(s) that led to your resentments?

Example:

      Coworkers—I made assumptions

      My spouse—I had unrealistic expectations

      My sponsor—I had unrealistic expectations and was impatient

_____

_____

_____

_____

_____

_____

_____

_____

If resentments are a problem for you, it may be helpful to do a daily inventory of your resentments and identify your role. You can only be accountable for you. Remember, it's your poison, not theirs.

Today I will let go of _____
Today, I will surrender it to my Higher Power.

Today I will let go of _____
Today, I will surrender it to my Higher Power.

Today I will let go of _____
Today, I will surrender it to my Higher Power.

Identifying resentments and then surrendering them to your Higher Power will help you let go of them. Each day, as you learn to release expectations, fears, and resentments, you learn to live life guided less by your own need to control people and situations, and more by your Higher Power.

Be accountable

Own responsibility

Let go

Today, I am grateful for _____

Multiple Forms
of Addiction

One, Two, Buckle My Shoe—Three, Four

To begin your journey in recovery, you first need to address your primary form of addiction. This is the addiction that is most potentially life-threatening. Many people struggle with more than one addiction. In early recovery, there is also a tendency to substitute one form of addiction for another. The perception may be that pot isn't as bad as cocaine, or watching internet porn is okay, but engaging with prostitutes is a problem, etc. Addicts tend to think obsessively and act compulsively, and that doesn't change just because you enter recovery.

The disease of addiction can create imbalance in areas of your life that may not have been problematic before. Perhaps you begin to work longer and longer hours, start to exercise compulsively, start or increase smoking, or adopt a variety of other addictive behaviors. So often, addiction manifests in unexpected areas of one's life. It is extremely important to be aware of this cycle because new areas of imbalance can become part of your addictive process, as well as potentially trigger a relapse of your primary addiction.

Feelings of shame that underlie many aspects of addiction frequently lead to secrecy, and the experience of being alone and isolated. The twelve-step saying, "We are only as sick as our secrets," speaks to the insidious effects of keeping secrets and the therapeutic value of sharing them as a way to promote healing and avoid relapse.

John told the following story regarding his multiple forms of addiction:

> "I began recovery for my drinking three years ago. I got a sponsor, prayed, meditated, and attended lots of meetings. I figured that doing these things would guarantee me ongoing sobriety, one day at a time. What I didn't know was that under the surface I

was also addicted to sex. Several times a week, I would have a few drinks after work at a local bar. At least once a week, I had sex with one of the people I met at the bar. When I began recovery for my drinking, I figured that I had been having anonymous sex just because I was drunk and lonely. I was wrong. Even though I was going to my Alcoholics Anonymous meetings, I found myself missing this anonymous sex more and more. I began to fantasize about having sex with strangers. I felt a great deal of shame about this and kept this whole area of my life secret from my sponsor and others in the program. I thought that they would think less of me or judge me. I told myself that I could control my behavior.

"I thought that maybe I could go back to my local bar and just drink club soda. Maybe I could just have conversations and not go home with one of these strangers. Before I knew it, I was back on my familiar barstool several times per week —cruising. I began going home with strangers, but it was much harder for me now, because without the alcohol I wasn't the smooth talker. That was when I relapsed with drinking. The first night I felt terrible, but ignored my feelings by having sex with a stranger. Very soon, I was drinking more than before and having anonymous sex almost every night of the week. Now, I see that underneath my addiction to alcohol was also an addiction to sex. I had deluded myself into believing that I was only a drunk and ignored my addiction to sex. My addiction to sex led me to relapse with alcohol. Today, I attend Alcoholics Anonymous and Sex Addicts Anonymous. I know that I need to be on the lookout for how, when, and where other forms of addiction may present themselves in my life."

Jim was extremely distraught about the consequences of his gambling. He had no doubt he was an addict. Every aspect of his life was negatively affected. One day, after a failed suicide attempt, he sought treatment. While he was no longer deluded in his thinking about the role gambling played in his life, and was sincere about wanting to stop, in four months he had relapsed three times. Each successive relapse was longer and accompanied by more severe consequences. Each relapse was also precipitated by his use of alcohol. He had been told to stop drinking for the sake of his recovery. It was only after these relapses that he recognized that, while he was further along in the progression of his addiction to gambling, he engaged in both gambling and drinking addictively. They were interactive, a package, and recovery from both would be necessary.

Lynn began to address her eating disorder—a cycle of compulsive overeating followed by self-starving, only after developing health problems that she could not ignore. She discovered that she was sexually avoidant during her overeating phase and acted out sexually in tandem with her self-starving. Her eating disorder and her addictive sexual behavior existed in tandem with each other. Addressing both forms of addiction was essential in order for her to recover.

If you identify yourself as an alcoholic, are you still using other drugs such as marijuana, cocaine, or prescription medication (without the complete knowledge of your physician, sponsor, and counselor)?

Yes ☐   No ☐

If you are recovering from other drugs, are you still using alcohol?

Yes ☐   No ☐

The following is a list of extremely common forms of addiction:
Alcohol, Other Drugs, Gambling, Spending
Risk—high risk sports, business ventures, dangerous activities
Sex
Pornography
Relationships
Work
Exercise
Self-starving
Compulsive overeating
Binge eating
Starving
Purging (via exercise, laxatives, vomiting, etc.)
Video gaming
Internet/social media

Have you ever wondered whether or not any of these were problematic for you?

Yes ☐   No ☐

Has anyone ever suggested that any of these could be problematic?

Yes ☐   No ☐

Have you used any of these to medicate or numb your feelings?

Yes ☐   No ☐

Do you engage in any of these to feel your feelings more?

      Yes ☐   No ☐

Have you engaged in efforts to control or stop any of these behaviors, only to resume them?

      Yes ☐   No ☐

Have you experienced financial, health, relationship, or family problems as a result?

      Yes ☐   No ☐

Do you think it would it be helpful to seek an outside opinion as to whether or not your recovery is threatened by your involvement in any of the above behaviors?

      Yes ☐   No ☐

What are you feeling as you answer these questions?

_____

_____

_____

If you believe that you have additional forms of addiction, it is important to seek immediate assistance to address them as part of your recovery.

- If you have a sponsor, talk to him or her about developing a plan of action.
- Find the twelve-step program most appropriate for the other form(s) of addiction.
- As necessary and appropriate, seek inpatient or outpatient treatment to address the other form(s) of addiction.

Able to identify and own multiple forms of addiction

Today, I am grateful for _____

Triggers

Triggers are specific memories, situations, and behaviors that have the potential to jeopardize your recovery. Pulling the trigger on a gun signals that a bullet is about to be fired. For people in recovery, triggers bring them closer to relapse.

John, who is in recovery from alcohol and sex addiction, describes his relapse as follows: "Even though I had quit drinking and acting out sexually, I still spent a lot of time in bars. Most of my business meetings were held in bars because that is where my clients preferred to meet. It became harder and harder for me not to order a drink or talk to attractive women. Finally one night, I gave in and ordered a drink. The next thing I remember was being at a motel with someone I didn't even know." For John, a significant trigger to re-engage in his addictive behaviors was the environment in which he spent time. His addictive thinking led him to believe that he was "strong enough" to resist his environment.

Although some triggers are unique to the individual, others are universal. One particularly strong trigger is euphoric recall. This is when you romanticize using behaviors and forget about the negative consequences. Susan, a compulsive overspender said, "When I first got into recovery, I spent a lot of time thinking about my spending sprees. I used to focus on one particular memory where I went on a $3,000 shopping trip to buy an entire new wardrobe. The more I thought about that spending spree, the more beautiful the clothes became, and I was tempted to go back out and start spending again. What I forgot about that $3,000 shopping trip was that it sent me into bankruptcy."

When you talk about your active addiction, do you tend to focus predominantly on the pleasurable or exciting times?

Yes ☐   No ☐

Do you tend to romanticize various using experiences?

Yes ☐   No ☐

When this continues, especially in early recovery, people often start to think how nice it might be to go back out "just one more time" and engage in their addictive behaviors again. *After all, how bad could it be? I'm in recovery now, right? If I just had a few drinks, just had an affair, just whatever, I'd be able to stop if I wanted to, wouldn't I?*

The answer is **NO**. Once people in recovery go "back out," their lives usually quickly disintegrate into the old madness of their addiction. This is how addiction works.

In the last month, have you experienced euphoric recall?

    Yes ☐   No ☐

In the last week, have you experienced euphoric recall?

    Yes ☐   No ☐

Identify how you engage in euphoric recall. Note the negative consequences that go with your idealized memory.

Euphoric Recall	Negative Consequences
Example: Hours spent in bar with friends	Two drinking and driving arrests
Example: Thrill in throwing the dice; making my point	Eventually I was the loser
Example: I saw myself looking good	I was a walking skeleton

Euphoric Recall	Negative Consequences

If you find yourself falling into euphoric recall, there are several important steps you can take:
- Immediately disengage from fantasizing and/or leave the situation.
- Call your sponsor. He or she will know what you are going through, because he or she has been there.
- Call someone in your twelve-step program. Reaching out to another addict can be an invaluable lifeline.
- Go to a meeting. Being able to share your experiences with others who understand and can empathize is healing and helps you remember why you are in recovery.

These steps come directly from the Emergency Plan described in detail in a later section. That is why it is important to have it with you at all times. You never know when it will be needed. Remember that the hardest day in recovery is always better than the best day out using.

Smell and taste can be triggers. The smell of beer or whiskey can be a trigger. The taste can be a trigger. This is why it is dangerous territory to drink "near beer" or non-alcoholic beer or wine.

Social stressors can be significant triggers for relapse. There may have been many situations, such as going to work, going on dates, to family picnics, in which you may have medicated yourself beforehand. These same situations present themselves in recovery. When you start to feel pressured and uncomfortable, the urge to return to your preferred form of addiction can feel overwhelming.

Other triggers include losses, such as important relationships—through breakup, divorce, and death. Maybe your relationship has recently broken up or someone close to you has passed away. In active addiction you would have numbed yourself to the pain of these kinds of losses. Now, maybe for the first time, you choose to face it as a person in recovery.

Are certain feelings triggers for you?

       Yes ☐   No ☐

Assess Potential Triggers

It is important to learn to self-assess for potential high-risk situations and triggers to relapse. Complete the following exercise:

Name triggers you are aware of	Identify actions you can take to lessen or remove your exposure to trigger
1)	
2)	
3)	
4)	
5)	

"Down time" and feeling empty are other areas that many people struggle with in recovery. Often, hours or days were spent each week engaging in addictive behaviors. Now, in recovery, it can feel as though there is a void.

Are there areas of your life you feel are empty now that you are in recovery?

1) _____

_____

2) _____

_____

3) _____

_____

What positive recovery-oriented activities can you engage in to fill this extra time and space?

1) _____

_____

2) _____

_____

3) _____

_____

Identify relapse triggers

Identify positive recovery activities

Today, I am grateful for _____

Relationships

The Helping Hand

All addicts have had enablers in their lives. These are people who, out of their care and love, "help" you in ways that make it easier to not feel the consequences of your behavior. Enablers buffer you from the effects of your addiction, which helps the addiction to continue.

- Marie is a compulsive gambler. Her parents pay her credit card bills so she won't have bad credit.
- Carole's husband seeks help from friends in the police department to reduce her drug charges.
- Cindy's mom and dad demand she switch schools when the athletic director tells them their daughter's fractures are related to an eating disorder.
- Charlie's dad buys him new cars and pays his college tuition even though Charlie can't keep a job, wrecks his cars, and drops his classes mid-term due to his substance use.
- Richard's wife ignores the phone calls from his many girlfriends, wondering why these women are trying to be so hurtful to her and her husband.

None of these caring people hold the addict accountable for his or her behavior. Identify your enablers and their enabling behavior.

Name _____

1) _____

2) _____

3) _____

4) _____

A Hole in the Sidewalk

Name _____

1) _____

2) _____

3) _____

4) _____

Name _____

1) _____

2) _____

3) _____

4) _____

Name _____

1) _____

2) _____

3) _____

4) _____

As a recovering addict, you need to learn to ask others to not assume responsibility for your behaviors. You need to meet your own wants and needs. Part of your recovery is being responsible and accountable for your actions. Approach your enablers and tell them their behavior (be specific) is not helping you and is actually getting in the way of your recovery. While others have probably told them this, they are more likely to believe it when they hear it directly from you. Take responsibility for whether or not you allow others to enable you.

Name your enablers again:

Name _____

Are you willing to quit relying on this person to enable you?

Yes ☐   No ☐

Name _____

Are you willing to quit relying on this person to enable you?

     Yes ☐   No ☐

Name _____

Are you willing to quit relying on this person to enable you?

     Yes ☐   No ☐

Name _____

Are you willing to quit relying on this person to enable you?

     Yes ☐   No ☐

You are accountable for your behavior. Recovery is about showing up and taking responsibility.

Identity enablers

Take responsibility for self and recovery

Today, I am grateful for _____

Trigger Relationships

Certain behaviors within relationships are serious relapse triggers. For Mike, working and traveling with his alcoholic father is a serious trigger for his own recovery from substance abuse. "It is extremely difficult for me to work and be around my father when he is actively engaging in his addiction. I am constantly confronted by my anger with him and my desire to use."

For Lori, a sex addict, being around her brother-in-law, with whom she acted out sexually, is a trigger. Being around her sister, with whom she has tremendous guilt, is also a trigger. "I feel so much shame and guilt when I am around them. I constantly think about my actions and beat myself up. Yet, I can't avoid them because they are part of my family."

For Kevin, returning to work where his co-workers and friends use drugs is a trigger. "How am I supposed to go back to work with these people? My whole social life with them is centered on drinking and using. We would use at lunch, after work, and on weekends. Without substances, how do I relate to these people?"

For Sherry, being around her father, who was her childhood perpetrator, triggers her eating disorder. "Whenever I see my dad, I feel so much anger, pain, and shame, that I medicate my feelings by eating. Then, I feel guilty for acting out in my eating disorder. It's a vicious cycle."

Identify the people that will be significant potential triggers for you.

1) _____

2) _____

3) _____

4) _____

What is it about your relationship with these people that is a trigger for you?

1) _____

2) _____

3) _____

When thinking of these relationships and their triggers, consider:

- Do you need to say some things directly to this person to set the stage for a different relationship?
- In what ways can you limit contact, if that is necessary to protect your recovery?
- What acts of self-care can you employ if you must see these people? Acts of self-care can be things you do before and after you have seen them, as well as what you do and say while with them. For example, you may want to talk with your sponsor prior to a visit. If this is a family reunion, you may choose to stay away from the specific areas where people are partying, and limit the amount of time you spend at the event. Another aspect of self-care is to know ahead of time what topics you are or are not willing to discuss.
- Would Al-Anon or Nar-Anon be a useful support? These are twelve-step programs for family members and friends of addicts.
- Identify other strategies that could be helpful for you.
- Talk to others in recovery about the successful strategies they have used in these kinds of situations.

Recent Relationships

Being in a painful primary relationship in which you do not take care of yourself is also a trigger. Sue, who is new to recovery from her eating disorder but doesn't address how her partner chronically berates her, is likely to relapse.

Name two people with whom you have had a recent painful relationship:

1) _____

2) _____

Think about the most of these two recent relationships and answer these questions: What hurtful behavior took place that you tolerated?

_____

_____

_____

What rationalizations did you use to accept that hurtful behavior and allow it to continue?

_____

_____

_____

In what ways did you take care of yourself?

_____

_____

_____

In what ways did you not take care of yourself?

_____

_____

_____

How were you hurtful toward the other person in the relationship?

_____

_____

_____

Repeat the same questions in regards to the second painful relationship.

What hurtful behavior took place that you tolerated?

_____

_____

_____

What rationalizations did you use to accept that hurtful behavior and allow it to continue?

_____

_____

_____

In what ways did you take care of yourself?

_____

_____

_____

In what ways did you not take care of yourself?

_____

_____

_____

How were you hurtful toward the other person in the relationship?

_____

_____

_____

Identify any patterns or similarities in your experience with these two relationships.

_____

_____

_____

It is essential to identify the aspects of your relationships that can be hurtful to your recovery. While you will not always be able to stop others from hurtful behavior, you are responsible for how you react to that behavior, and whether or not you accept it.

Identify trigger relationships

Plan for self-care

Today, I am grateful for _____

Relationship View

People who come from dysfunctional families and who struggle with addiction go through much of their lives making assumptions or guessing about what is normal or what is appropriate in relationships. Because of a lack of healthy models, they are frequently operating in a vacuum. The following characteristics offer a healthy framework for relationships.

Respect
Respect is a fundamental acceptance of who you are, your autonomy, and your uniqueness. Respect is an attitude for which courtesy is an expression.

Honesty
Honesty and open communication mean that people are free to be themselves. "I have given up fear of rejection when I am less than perfect, when I am vulnerable, when it may mean you disagree with me. I can tell you my feelings, my thoughts, without fear of a major catastrophe."

Realistic Expectations
You need to be realistic about what you can offer others and what they can offer you. A history of growing up with enmeshed boundaries, having unrealistic expectations placed on you, or wishful thinking on your part, can lead to unrealistic expectations of others and yourself. Be aware that other people are not going to be available to meet all of your needs—nor should they. Be cautious of any one person trying to meet all of your needs at all times. That person is likely very controlling and/or very fearful of rejection, has difficulty taking responsibility for themselves, and hasn't developed a healthy sense of self.

Trust
Trust means, "I feel physically and psychologically safe with you. I have neither fears nor anxieties with respect to your treatment of me." In order for there to be trust in a relationship, there needs to be consistency, predictability, and a demonstrated reliability that a person will follow through with their intentions—that what he or she does is consistent with what he or she says. Trust is like a brick wall—it takes time to build.

Autonomy
Intimacy is a sharing of autonomy. Real autonomy means that each of us takes responsibility for our own lives, and for evolving into the best human being we can be. We fulfill our own life scripts and exercise our own physical, emotional, and spiritual energies. With autonomy we have the ability to

be clear about our own needs, while respecting the boundaries and choices of others, and honoring their individual differences.

However, it is important to be cautious in that autonomy sometimes passes for unbridled, unmitigated selfishness. *To hell with the rest of the world, I am going to get what I want when I want it, because I am autonomous.* No one is entitled to get what he or she wants when he or she wants it, regardless of circumstance.

While a healthy relationship is not a power struggle between two rigidly autonomous beings, neither should it be symbiotic. The two of you do not have to think and feel the same way about everything. The two of you want to share yourselves with each other without collapsing into one being.

Shared Power

A healthy relationship is about shared power, rather than control. Both people in the relationship are able to take initiative and to respond freely. There is a mutual give and take. They relinquish the need to be right and eliminate the idea of "ownership." There is mutuality and reciprocity in the relationship.

The notion of shared power with children is often a problem for parents. However, when children feel powerless, there are usually very negative consequences for both parents and their children. While parents need to operate from a position of authority, and are responsible for providing healthy structure and boundaries, they can, nonetheless, offer children age-appropriate areas of mutual power sharing.

Tenderness

Tenderness is demonstrated with physical affection. This is the kind of nonsexual physical touching we all need to thrive. There is nurturing touch that says, "I am here; you are not alone." "I offer you my support." "Hello."

Tenderness is also expressed in words and attitude. In your longest-standing relationships, you may find it easy to discontinue the little niceties you offer those you don't know as well. Over time, it can become easy to take your partners, your parents, and even your friends for granted. It is essential to strive to not fall into this pattern.

Time

Relationships need time. When 150 couples in committed relationships (living together for over four years) were asked how much time they spent with their partner each day, the average was twenty-three minutes. Twenty-three minutes with the person each considered the most important to his or her life! People grow apart for many reasons, but for some it is as simple as getting caught up in other responsibilities and not making time to "be" in the relationship. Valued relationships deserve your time.

Long-Term Commitment

To have a healthy relationship you need to pay attention to the relationship's dynamics and make a commitment to working on your part. In a healthy relationship, you trust that if there are problems, the two of you will work them out. You trust that when there are problems, it does not mean the relationship is over.

Commitment does not mean you stay in a relationship regardless of what may occur. At times, as people change, relationships are renegotiated and commitments become stronger or weaker. When people make a commitment to a relationship, they do what they can to make it work. However, they do not allow themselves to be abused or give up their integrity in the process.

Forgiveness

There has to be room for forgiveness in any relationship. Forgiveness does not mean selling your heart, soul, or integrity to have peace. It means remembering and letting go. It is a cleansing of your pain and anger. It means maintaining your integrity while being able to let go of the hurt, anger, resentment, and pain you have held onto.

Charting a Relationship

The following is an example of how Tom sees his relationship with his seventeen-year-old son, using these relationship characteristics. On this scale, a score of one means the least of the characteristic and a score of ten means the most.

Characteristic	1	2	3	4	5	6	7	8	9	10
Respect	X									
Honesty			X							
Realistic Expectations			X							
Trust		X								
Autonomy		X								
Shared Power				X						
Tenderness				X						
Time				X						
Long-Term Commitment								X		
Forgiveness				X						

Clearly, this relationship is struggling. It takes a lot of honesty to benefit from this exercise, and Tom realized that he was still angry with his son for not actively pursuing a particular sport, football, in combination with his son's emotional sensitivity and orientation to music. As a result, Tom realized the crux to establishing a better relationship with his son was for him to work on allowing his son greater autonomy and respecting his interest, choices, and individuality. He recognized that he needed to own the loss of never having been the great athlete he wanted to be. Tom acknowledged that it was more important to know his son for who he really is than to try to control him.

Charting a Relationship

Think of someone with whom you have a significant relationship. On a scale of one to ten, in which a score of one means the least of each characteristic and a score of ten the most, chart this relationship.

Name _____

Respect

| 1 | 2 | 3 | 4 | 5 | 6 | 7 | 8 | 9 | 10 |

Honesty

| 1 | 2 | 3 | 4 | 5 | 6 | 7 | 8 | 9 | 10 |

Realistic Expectations

| 1 | 2 | 3 | 4 | 5 | 6 | 7 | 8 | 9 | 10 |

Trust

| 1 | 2 | 3 | 4 | 5 | 6 | 7 | 8 | 9 | 10 |

Autonomy

| 1 | 2 | 3 | 4 | 5 | 6 | 7 | 8 | 9 | 10 |

Shared Power

| 1 | 2 | 3 | 4 | 5 | 6 | 7 | 8 | 9 | 10 |

Tenderness

| 1 | 2 | 3 | 4 | 5 | 6 | 7 | 8 | 9 | 10 |

Time

| 1 | 2 | 3 | 4 | 5 | 6 | 7 | 8 | 9 | 10 |

Long-Term Commitment

| 1 | 2 | 3 | 4 | 5 | 6 | 7 | 8 | 9 | 10 |

Forgiveness

| 1 | 2 | 3 | 4 | 5 | 6 | 7 | 8 | 9 | 10 |

Now that you have completed the exercise, identify short-term, intermediate, and long-range goals for what you can do to improve this relationship.

Short-term goals

1) _____

2) _____

3) _____

Intermediate goals

1) _____

2) _____

3) _____

Long-term goals

1) _____

2) _____

3) _____

Identify healthy criteria for relationships

Be accountable for self in relationships

Today, I am grateful for _____

Warning Signs

Watch Your Step

Imagine pilots preparing a plane for takeoff. They perform a rigorous examination of the plane and go through a checklist before each flight to ensure the safety of everyone on the flight. Should anything problematic be found, they have specific procedures to address the situation. Recovery is much the same. By having a warning signs checklist, you can monitor whether or not any addictive behaviors, patterns, or signs of relapse are occurring. Sponsors and significant others can also be an excellent source of feedback in helping to monitor potential trouble spots. Obviously, this does not mean they are responsible for your recovery. It means that perhaps they have a more objective view and can see things in your behavior that you may not be able to see.

Warning Signs Checklist

The following Warning Signs Checklist will help to monitor your behavior. Should problematic behaviors start to occur, you will have a specific plan to address the warning signs.

Fill out the following checklist, circling the number that applies to you currently. On this scale of one to ten, one means that you least identify with the statement and ten means that you most identify with it.

Statement	1	2	3	4	5	6	7	8	9	10
I have no interest in doing things	1	2	3	4	5	6	7	8	9	10
I have no interest in my appearance	1	2	3	4	5	6	7	8	9	10
I am discouraged about the future	1	2	3	4	5	6	7	8	9	10
I have trouble sleeping	1	2	3	4	5	6	7	8	9	10
I rarely see my friends	1	2	3	4	5	6	7	8	9	10
I rarely go to twelve-step meetings	1	2	3	4	5	6	7	8	9	10
I rarely see my sponsor	1	2	3	4	5	6	7	8	9	10

I eat very little	1	2	3	4	5	6	7	8	9	10
I am distant from my family/friends	1	2	3	4	5	6	7	8	9	10
I don't enjoy activities	1	2	3	4	5	6	7	8	9	10
I believe I could use or engage in addictive behavior	1	2	3	4	5	6	7	8	9	10
I believe I can control my addiction	1	2	3	4	5	6	7	8	9	10
I am very aggressive	1	2	3	4	5	6	7	8	9	10
I feel like I need to control things	1	2	3	4	5	6	7	8	9	10
I don't like to listen to others	1	2	3	4	5	6	7	8	9	10
I feel resentful	1	2	3	4	5	6	7	8	9	10
My relationships are toxic	1	2	3	4	5	6	7	8	9	10
I have lots of secrets	1	2	3	4	5	6	7	8	9	10
I feel ashamed	1	2	3	4	5	6	7	8	9	10
I feel depressed and worthless	1	2	3	4	5	6	7	8	9	10

Now that you have completed this checklist, describe what you see.

_____

_____

_____

Are there any patterns that you can identify?

_____

_____

_____

For any questions on which you answered six or higher, what specific behaviors can you engage in to help prevent relapse?

Examples:

Warning Sign	Preventative Behavior
No interest in my appearance	When I dress in the morning, dress with the attitude that clean clothes represent clean recovery. Throw or give away pants with holes. Wash clothes twice weekly.

Recognize relapse warnings

Identify self-care strategies

Today, I am grateful for _____

Spirituality

Came . . . Came to . . . Came to Believe

More people have achieved recovery through twelve-step programs than through any other single resource, and all twelve-step programs have a spiritual component. The willingness to accept a Higher Power is often a stumbling block for addicts seeking recovery. Step Two of the Twelve Steps is, *"Came to believe that a Power greater than ourselves could restore us to sanity."*

As the phrase "Came to believe," suggests, spiritual discovery is a journey. In terms of your spiritual journey, you do not need to feel as though you should have already arrived or that you need to arrive by a certain time or date. Your sense of journey may have already begun. It may be about to start. The important point is that you have a willing spirit.

Spiritual Vision

Complete the following exercise.

Do you believe there is a power greater than yourself?

Yes ☐   No ☐

Explain:

_____

_____

_____

_____

_____

To heal from pain and conflict in your life, you need to have faith in something outside of yourself. For many people, the faith may be in a Higher Power or God. Others aren't sure. While you may be agnostic or have little faith in anything outside yourself, if you can be open to letting go of the need to control and try to develop faith, your recovery will benefit. Trust that in time, healing and self-love will become a part of your life.

If you are experiencing conflict with this aspect of recovery, answers to the following questions may offer some important insights.

Did you attend a church, synagogue, or another house of worship as a child? If so, name and describe. If not, what was the message in your family about this area of life?

_____

_____

_____

If you were involved in a particular faith as a child, was it:

Fun?	☐ Yes	☐ No
Scary?	☐ Yes	☐ No
Boring?	☐ Yes	☐ No
Meaningful?	☐ Yes	☐ No

Was your concept of God:

Loving?	☐ Yes	☐ No
Punishing?	☐ Yes	☐ No
Indifferent?	☐ Yes	☐ No
Other?	☐ Yes	☐ No

Did you have a choice about whether or not you attended a church, synagogue, etc.?

Yes ☐   No ☐

If you have discontinued being involved with the faith with which you grew up, how was that decision made?

_____

_____

_____

As a child or teenager, were there any particular rituals or ceremonies that were of special significance for you?

Yes ☐   No ☐

What were they?

_____

_____

_____

What made them special for you?

_____

_____

What does your Higher Power look like at this time? (You are welcome to describe this in words or draw or picture below.)

_____

_____

_____

_____

_____

_____

_____

_____

_____

Now that you have completed these questions, what thoughts or reflections do you have?

_____

_____

_____

_____

_____

_____

_____

Recognize impact of spiritual history

Create vision of a Higher Power

Today, I am grateful for _____

Packing for the Spiritual Journey

In the famous poem, *Footprints in the Sand,* a man describes a dream he had wherein he was walking along a beach with his Higher Power. As scenes from all phases of his life flashed before his eyes, he noticed that for most of these scenes there were two sets of footprints in the sand—one belonging to him and other to his Higher Power. However, as he looked back on the path he had walked during his life, he saw that there were times when there was only a single set of footprints. He noticed that the single set of footprints coincided with his most difficult and painful experiences.

He interpreted this as his Higher Power abandoning him during these challenging times. He asked his Higher Power why he was left by himself during the times he most needed help and guidance. The answer he received was that, contrary to being abandoned, during those times he was carried by his Higher Power.

Identify three times in your life you believe you were carried.

1) _____

2) _____

3) _____

Spiritual growth is a journey that continues throughout your lifetime. When your spiritual life is out of balance, so are the other important aspects of your life. A belief in a Higher Power rarely comes instantly. It does not strike like a lightning bolt. Faith is achieved through one's daily activities. Just like your physical body requires regular exercise and proper diet to maintain your health, your spirituality needs regular nourishment and exercise to remain healthy.

Step Two can be broken down into the following pieces:

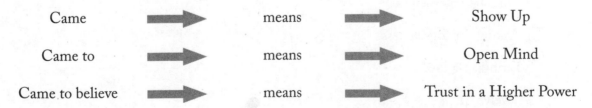

Came	means	Show Up
Came to	means	Open Mind
Came to believe	means	Trust in a Higher Power

Step Two is achieved by taking small, calming steps on an enlightening journey. The journey does not lead to a destination or end point called spiritual life. Rather, there are many spiritual rewards along the path. The payoff comes in making the journey, rather than reaching a specific destination.

Spiritual Journey

The exercise below is designed to increase your awareness about your own spiritual pathways. Check all the experiences that describe your spiritual journey.

- ☐ Music/singing
- ☐ Quiet, solitude
- ☐ Appreciating nature
- ☐ Loving others unselfishly
- ☐ Listening to others
- ☐ Sharing your feelings
- ☐ Keeping a journal
- ☐ Forgiving others
- ☐ Attending a church, synagogue, or other place of worship
- ☐ Praising others
- ☐ Smiling, laughing
- ☐ Reading, learning
- ☐ Helping others
- ☐ Sharing experiences
- ☐ Asking for forgiveness
- ☐ Embracing loved ones
- ☐ Twelve Steps
- ☐ Meditation
- ☐ Other spiritual practice

What makes these pathways important to you?

_____

_____

_____

_____

_____

_____

_____

What things in your life interfere with your spiritual journey?

_____

_____

_____

Write a want ad for the Higher Power that you would like to have in your life. Ideally, a Higher Power should be someone or something you can trust and that can help you.

_____

_____

_____

_____

Name five other qualities or characteristics you would look for in a Higher Power.

1) _____

2) _____

A Hole in the Sidewalk

3) _____

4) _____

5) _____

Achieve greater serenity

Increase clarity of spiritual path

Today, I am grateful for _____

Secrets

Behind Closed Doors

Relapse can be a consequence of hanging on to secrets. Common secrets of people with addiction include past sexual activities, criminal activities, other addictive behaviors, sexual orientation, financial difficulties, and/or other areas of life that may feel too shameful or painful to reveal to others.

- James, conflicted about telling his home group he was gay, eventually relapsed in his eating disorder.
- Susan, after nine months of recovery from her cocaine addiction, relapsed when her boyfriend threatened to tell her husband of their affair.
- Gary had been in recovery from heroin addiction for seven years, with the help of a twelve-step program. But he continued to secretly gamble, creating more and more debt that he kept hidden from his family. Unable to cope with the stress of his gambling debts and having to lie about it, he resumed his use of drugs.
- Tina has been in recovery for three years but when her daughter turned eight she relapsed. When Tina was eight, her father molested her. This is a memory she had previously repressed which had now become conscious, overwhelming her.
- Sam is in recovery from sex addiction. He never disclosed a previous prostitution charge while he was active in his disease. The fear his wife will discover his secret led to his relapse.

Secrets are defined as information that is:

    Kept hidden or concealed

    Dependably discreet

    Operating in a hidden or confidential manner

    Not expressed

As children, most people learned what secrets were and how to keep them. As a child, you played and interacted with friends and family, often learned that secrets were fun to keep. When you learned information that others may not have known, you felt special and important. But most addicts are raised in troubled families where hurtful secrets abound.

As a child you may have been solicited to keep secrets that made you feel as if you were doing something wrong or shameful. Perhaps you saw your mother or father pouring alcohol into their morning coffee or orange juice. Your parent might have said, "Be mommy or daddy's big boy or girl and don't tell anyone about this." This put you in a situation where you were asked to keep a secret that you may or may not have known was wrong to keep. In this situation, most children experience a great deal of internal conflict—they are worried about the possible harmful consequences of not telling someone else, but don't want their parent to be angry with them, so they keep the secret.

The circumstances of your situation may have been different. Maybe you kept the secret from your friends that your family member(s) had an addiction. Maybe the secret was about mom or dad having an affair. Whatever the case, the end results were the same. You felt afraid that your parents or someone else significant in your life would be angry with you. If this happened, you probably feared that you would be punished, hit, or yelled at for not keeping their secret(s). Many people learn to keep secrets so well as children, that today they often still carry some of them.

As a child, you may have learned how secrets work in an overt and/or covert manner. You may have been explicitly told not to talk to anyone else about things that happened within your family. "My mother used to come and cry in my bedroom at night after my father hit her," Mary confessed. When I would ask why she wouldn't leave him or report him to the police, my mother would quickly compose herself. She would tell me, 'your father just has a small problem with his anger. I don't want anything bad to happen to him.'" In Mary's family, she learned overtly that she had to be the keeper of the family secret and the family shame.

In Ron's family keeping the secret was more covert. "Sometimes after school, my friends would come over to play. By this time of the day, my dad had been drinking for several hours. Often, he would be passed out on the couch when my friends and I came home after school. When my friends would ask what was wrong with my dad, I would say he had a migraine headache and had to take medication. No one ever had to tell me that I needed to make excuses for my dad. I instinctively knew that was what I had to do." Ron became the keeper of the family secret and the family shame.

There is a distinction between a confidence and a secret. When children are asked to keep the details of a surprise birthday party or vacation from others, they are being asked to keep a confidence. If others found out, there may be disappointment or loss of the surprise element. They keep this information confidential because they want to, not because they felt as though they had to.

Children often instinctively know that keeping secrets is not even a choice. It is a matter of personal or family survival. They are being asked to contain the emotional energy and shame embodied in the secret within the family. There could be overwhelming negative consequences if others found out the secret. Such secrets are handed down from one generation to another. Secrets are pieces of information that are withheld from others, often out of shame, and many times with the intent to protect someone—yourself or another. Secrets are powerful because they can control you. Very often, the primary problem of a secret is not its content, but what you must do to keep the secret.

Two examples of secrets in my family of origin are:

1) _____

2) _____

It was important for me to keep these secrets because:

1) _____

2) _____

What I had to do to keep these secrets was (specific actions):

_____

_____

_____

Secrets carry a great deal of power and weight. An individual in a family system is confronted with the content of the secret and having to keep the secret from family members, friends, and society. Carrying a secret is a tremendous burden. There is a great deal of shame inherent in having to keep certain secrets. As a keeper of the family's secret(s), you may have felt shame regarding the family member the secret was about and yourself. You may have felt that your value as a person was in question by being a member of such a family.

Many people have held on to secrets from their history for extended periods of time to avoid shame and possible social or legal consequences. By keeping these secrets, you are reinforcing your inner core of shame. Shame is the inner belief that you have little or no value as a person. Having a shame core means that feeling that you are worthless.

When your shame core is triggered, your emotional and spiritual pain can become so great that you need to re-engage in your addictive behaviors as a form of self-medication. Letting go of your secrets is crucial to staying in recovery and preventing relapse.

What secrets are you carrying today? If the word "secret" seems too strong, what is it no one else knows about you that you would feel ashamed or embarrassed about if they knew?

1) _____

2) _____

3) _____

4) _____

5) _____

6) _____

7) _____

8) _____

Specific personal secrets I would like to release are:

1) _____

2) _____

3) _____

4) _____

5) _____

6) _____

7) _____

8) _____

Completing this exercise took a tremendous amount of courage. It takes strength to move from a place of secrecy to taking action to be free of secrets. Remember that the sharing of secrets is not all-or-nothing ("I've never told anyone, now I need to tell everyone"). It is important to be able to decide who is and who is not appropriate to release secrets to.

These questions may be helpful in determining the appropriateness of revealing particular secrets.

> What secret would you like to share?
> With whom do you want to share this secret?
> Why do you want to share this information with this person?
> What do you hope will be the result?
> How realistic is that expectation?
> If the expectation is unrealistic, what is a more realistic expectation?

When wanting to release secrets, it is often very helpful to ask your sponsor and/or therapist to help you go through the above questions. When you have answered them, you can then begin to plan the appropriate circumstances under which to reveal your secret(s).

Here are some helpful guidelines for releasing secrets:
- Clarify that releasing the secret is for your benefit and not to get even with someone.
- Think through the potential consequences of releasing the secret.
- Think of how detailed you want your disclosure to be.
- Make sure the details of the secret to be revealed are correct to the best of your knowledge.
- Write out a plan for sharing the secret. Where? When? And with whom?

Disclosure about one's addictive behavior is vital in recovery. Yet, it is not suggested that one discloses without the assistance of a sponsor or a professional addictions counselor to help you determine what is and is not appropriate.

Identify with whom do you need to share more openly. Write down their names.

_____

_____

What feelings come up as you think about the secrets you've been carrying? (Examples include pain, fear, loneliness, anger, guilt, and shame.)

_____

_____

_____

_____

_____

What thoughts and feelings came up for you while completing this exercise?

_____

_____

_____

_____

_____

Please remember that as you get honest about your secrets, many feelings may come up:

    Pain about past abuses you have suffered

    Fear about what will happen if you tell others about the secret(s)

    Anger about being abused; guilt about being abusive

    Guilt about your past behaviors and mistakes

    Shame that if others know your secrets they will know you are worthless

Several tools can be used to support you when you are feeling overwhelmed with these and other feelings:

- Go to a meeting—this is an excellent place to share and feel supported without conditions
- Talk to your sponsor—he or she can offer perspective and support
- Talk to your therapist—she or he can also help to explore issues and be supportive
- Pray—talking to your Higher Power reminds you that you are not alone—now or ever
- Meditate—to help you to feel more grounded and calm
- Say positive affirmations—to focus on positive self-statements rather than negative ones

Now that you are becoming more aware of your secrets and what it costs you to keep them, you may have the urge to "tell all" to family members, children, spouses, and others. You may want to be sure that you don't spend even one more day hanging on to these secrets.

But, revealing all of your secrets can be damaging—to others and yourself. Certain secrets may be appropriate to reveal immediately, while others may not be appropriate to reveal to certain people at this time, if ever.

Distinguish difference between a confidence and a secret

Recognize role of secrets

Identify secrets important to share

Identify healthy guidelines for revealing secrets

Today, I am grateful for _____

Daily Schedule

Suit Up and Show Up

Many people with addiction are accustomed to a life filled with chaos and unpredictability. For some, this is the way life has always been, coming from a home environment filled with turmoil, addiction, abuse, and a variety of other challenges. Whether or not that was a part of your early life experiences, the rule today may be that there are no rules. Each day has no plan and is punctuated with stress, high excitement, and little or no time to get things done. Many addicts like living on the edge, and become addicted to the rush of the chaos.

A life in recovery means living a balanced life—a life with some structure and moderation. It means no longer living moment to moment in the insanity that surrounds addiction. Instead, you move toward trying to live a more serene and calm life, which nurtures your ongoing recovery. To do this, you need to learn how to schedule and plan.

This doesn't mean that every waking moment needs to be controlled and accounted for. It means having a flexible plan for what your day may look like and how recovery will be factored into it. You only need to plan *One Day at a Time*. Knowing your schedule helps to identify how much time is to be spent working, focusing on relationships, in leisure activities, and where recovery fits in.

Take a look at your schedule. Describe your average day in detail.

Today, when I first wake up, I

_____

_____

_____

To get ready for my day, I

_____

_____

_____

Continue to describe what your day looks like during the following times—where you are, who you are with, and what you are doing.

9:00 a.m.–Noon _____

_____

_____

Noon–3:00 p.m. _____

_____

_____

3:00–5:00 p.m. _____

_____

_____

5:00–7:00 p.m. _____

_____

_____

7:00–9:00 p.m. _____

_____

_____

9:00 p.m. until bedtime _____

_____

_____

Bedtime _____

_____

_____

Looking at the previous two days:

How much time was devoted to your recovery practice (twelve-step meetings, reading recovery literature, meditation, talking to others in recovery)?

_____

_____

_____

Were you able to get your recovery needs met?

_____

_____

_____

Did your behavior demonstrate that recovery was your number one priority? Explain.

_____

_____

_____

_____

_____

Were there any significant aspects of your life that you were not able to give time to?

_____

_____

_____

Identify any large periods of unaccounted for time. Your addiction often consumed a great deal of your time. Now that you are in recovery, you may have large gaps in your day. Laying out a schedule can help you to see that these spaces need to be filled with positive activities that support your recovery. Use this daily log as a way to monitor how you balance your day for the next week.

Finally, ask yourself these questions:

On a daily basis, what do I need to do to maintain my recovery?

_____

_____

_____

_____

_____

_____

_____

Specifically, what do I need to do today to stay in recovery?

_____

_____

_____

_____

_____

_____

_____

_____

_____

Make recovery my first priority

Be accountable to your practice of recovery

Today, I am grateful for _____

Priorities

First Things First

Using the circle below, divide it into pieces representing your specific priorities in life. For example, if your job and family were of equal importance in your life, and there were no other priorities, then each would have an equal half of the circle.

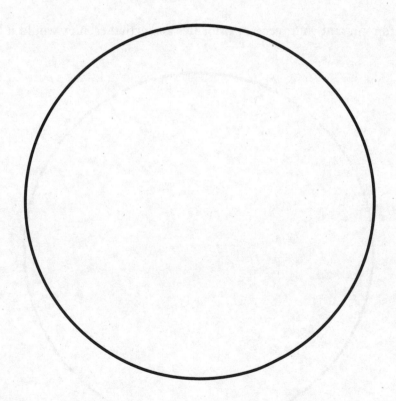

Now that you have divided the circle based on your priorities, what piece or pieces are the largest?

_____

A Hole in the Sidewalk

What piece or pieces are the smallest?

_____

How large a piece is your program of recovery?

_____

How does the way your circle is divided need to change to support your recovery?

_____

_____

_____

If this circle were to represent your recovery priorities and activities, how would it be divided?

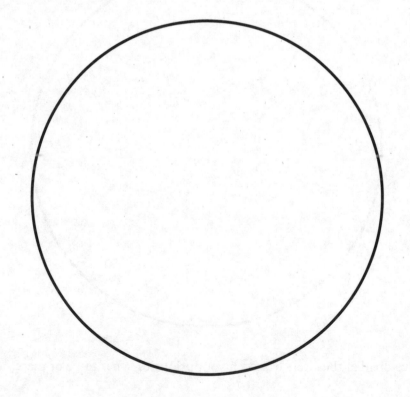

How large a piece represents time spent attending twelve-step/recovery meetings?

_____

How large a piece would represent time spent reading recovery-related materials?

_____

How large a piece would represent time spent meditating and connecting with your Higher Power?

_____

How large a piece would represent time spent with your sponsor and socializing with others in twelve-step recovery?

_____

The purpose of this exercise is to help identify where and how recovery fits in your life. For many addicts, recovery is not the number one priority. Similarly, you may find yourself focusing on other aspects of life that were neglected due to your addiction and prioritize them over recovery practice. Sometimes people become complacent about what it takes to maintain recovery. In order to prevent relapse, focusing on recovery *one day at a time* needs to be the most important priority in your life. Whatever you prioritize over your recovery—job, school, family, etc.—places your recovery in serious potential jeopardy. And, that places all of your other priorities in potential jeopardy. Consider, what would happen to your job, family, or school, etc., if you were to relapse?

What would a realistic list of priorities for you look like now?

1) _____

2) _____

3) _____

4) _____

5) _____

6) _____

7) _____

8) _____

What will help you to keep recovery your number one priority?

_____

_____

_____

_____

_____

Recognize priorities

Prioritize recovery practice

Today, I am grateful for _____

Meditation

Peace of Mind

One of the most healing elements of the twelve-step programs is the connection with your Higher Power. It connects you to yourself, to others, to your spirituality and to a power greater than you. Prayer and meditation are two excellent tools that increase this connection.

Remember that your relationship with your Higher Power is your own. Through prayer and meditation, you can establish a rich relationship that helps nourish your ongoing recovery.

There are a number of excellent books on meditation available. These include:
- *Step by Step*, Muriel Zink, Ballantine Books
- *May I Sit With You: A Simple Approach to Meditation*, Tom Catton, Central Recovery Press
- *Each Day a New Beginning: Daily Meditations for Women*, Hazelden Publications
- *Touchstones: Daily Meditations for Men*, Hazelden Publications
- *The Promise of a New Day*, Karen Casey, Martha Vanceburg, Hazelden Publications
- *Day by Day*, Hazelden Publications
- *The Wisdom of a Meaningful Life: The Essence of Mindfulness*, John Bruna, Central Recovery Press

There are many ways to meditate and guided meditations can be helpful for those beginning a mediation practice. There are many varieties of guided meditation available online and in MP3 format, as well as on CD. You may also appreciate Claudia Black's *Imageries* and *Letting Go Imageries*.

Below is an example of a spirituality meditation and visualization. Remember that this is only one way to meditate, not the way. The process of meditation may feel awkward at first if you haven't experienced it before, but it can be highly valuable. All you need to do is allow yourself to relax and be open to the process. Read it through a few times, then try it. You might also record it to your own selection of music.

A Hole in the Sidewalk

Find a comfortable sitting position, uncross your arms and legs, and begin to take slow deep breaths in and out. Gently sit back and close your eyes.

Begin to breathe slowly and deeply.

Focus on your breathing.

Take a deep breath in . . . and out.

Take a deep breath in . . . and out.

As you breathe in, visualize your Higher Power filling you with healing energy and protective light.

As you breathe out, visualize stress, tension, worry, and fear leaving your body. Continue to breathe in and out. Slowly become aware of your head and neck.
Feel your tension melting away and feel your head and neck begin to relax.

Feel this relaxation slowly moving down through your shoulders as you continue to breathe in healing light and energy.
Feel the relaxation move down into your arms and chest.
Know that you are safe and you are loved.
Breathe in . . . and out.
Breathe in . . . and out.
Feel the relaxation moving down into your waist and legs.
Feel the tension and stress leaving your body.
Feel the relaxation moving down into your feet.

Feel your connection to the earth and the connection to your Higher Power.
As you continue to breathe deeply, imagine a place where you feel completely safe and serene. This may be the mountains, the beach, the forest.

Wherever this place is, it is your place to be. Imagine yourself there right now. Take a look around and notice what you see.

What do you smell?

What do you hear?

Let all of your senses experience the serenity and safety of this special place. Know that this is your place that you can come to at any time.
Slowly begin to visualize how your Higher Power might look and feel.
Let the image begin to fill your mind, body, and spirit.

Imagine your body and spirit being filled with serenity, contentment, and peace.
Feel your spirit connecting with your Higher Power.
Feel the infinite wisdom and love your Higher Power has for you.

Feel the safety and protection it offers you.
Know that your Higher Power guides your path in recovery and is with you at all times.
Know that you can connect with your Higher Power and your safe place any time you choose through prayer and meditation.
Know that you are not alone in your recovery.

You are surrounded by love and support if you choose to let it in.
As you continue to breathe, gently become aware of your body.

Become aware of your head . . . your neck . . . your shoulders, and arms.
Become aware of your back . . . your chest . . . your waist . . . your legs, and your feet.
Become aware of your connection to the Earth.

When you are ready, open your eyes.

Use tools to facilitate meditation and prayer

Today, I am grateful for _____

Abstinence vs. Sobriety

Good vs. Best

Many addicts ask, "What is the difference between abstinence and recovery?"

Abstinence means that you have simply stopped engaging in your addictive behaviors. In addition to refraining from your addictive behaviors, recovery is engaging in a healthy lifestyle that promotes growth and healing.

When people only stop their using behaviors without getting into a program of recovery, all of the remaining aspects of their lives where they experience problems stay the same—nothing else changes. This is where the expression "dry drunk" comes from. An alcoholic stops drinking, but continues on in his or her insane and chaotic behavior because he or she is not using any new approaches or tools for living.

When you make a conscious choice to stop your addictive behaviors, on some level you have decided that you want a life free from the pain and chaos of compulsive drinking, drugging, eating, sex, gambling, etc. Recovery is abstaining from your addictive behaviors, *and* refraining from distorted and addictive thinking. It is learning skills that help you to live differently.

In recovery, people come to experience that life does not have to be characterized by pain and chaos. This doesn't mean that life won't have its trying moments. There is a recovery saying that speaks to how you can have serenity, even during difficult and challenging times:

Recovery doesn't always mean safety from the storm. It means safety during the storm.

In what areas of my life am I abstinent?

_____

_____

_____

In what areas of my life am I in recovery?

_____

_____

_____

In what ways can I improve my recovery?

_____

_____

_____

In what ways can I improve my serenity?

_____

_____

_____

Distinguish abstinence from recovery

Today, I am grateful for _____

Emergency Plan

But Wait . . . There's More

Now that you have completed this guide, and in light of what you are learning about yourself, what are the relapse warning signs and signals you need to watch for? Remember that knowledge of how your own addictive process works is a powerful tool you can use in your recovery. The more understanding you have about the specific factors that can lead to relapse, the more prepared you will be to create support systems and resources that help you protect and maintain your recovery.

Even in recovery, the disease of addiction continues to distort thinking, fueled by denial and minimization, about the potential for relapse. It is extremely important to identify your specific relapse warning signs and have a solid relapse prevention plan. If the warning signs begin to appear, you do not need spend a lot of time thinking about what to do, you need to act immediately and call upon the supportive resources you identified earlier.

Imagine this:

You are living in your house, apartment, etc., and you have thought ahead to what you would do in case of emergencies such as fire, flood, tornado, hurricane, or earthquake. You have a very specific plan in the event that any one of these situations should occur. Now, imagine that one of these situations is actually occurring. You would not stand around and engage in extended analysis, you would take immediate action to protect yourself and save your life. Think of relapse prevention in the same way. You need a specific plan to protect your life in recovery should you find yourself in harm's way.

Identify what you believe to be your most critical relapse warning signs.

1) _____

2) _____

3) _____

4) _____

Now list what you need to do to prevent a relapse if/when these signals occur. Be specific.

1) _____

2) _____

3) _____

4) _____

5) _____

6) _____

7) _____

8) _____

Identify six names and phone numbers of people you could call, should you experience a serious relapse trigger. Be realistic—identify those you are likely to be able to reach.

Name	Phone Number
1)	
2)	
3)	
4)	
5)	
6)	

What will you do if you cannot reach these contacts?

_____

_____

_____

Are you carrying a twelve-step meeting list in your car, your motorcycle, bicycle? Do you have one at home, work, and school?

_____

If you were to relapse, whom will you call? Do not just consider a relapse the resumption of your addiction, but also the self-defeating behavior that is a relapse trigger.

Name	Phone Number
1)	
2)	
3)	
4)	
5)	
6)	

Make sure that you keep this relapse emergency plan with you at all times. In order for your emergency plan to work, you need access to it.

An Emergency Plan only works if you put it into action immediately when you begin to see warning signs. They may even be small warning signs like attending fewer meetings, not calling your sponsor as often, an increase in controlling behavior, a heightened attitude of over confidence, hanging onto resentments, etc. Whatever the signs may be, these are precisely the times that you need the plan to help protect your precious recovery.

Identify critical relapse contributors

Have specific Emergency Plan

Today, I am grateful for _____

A Hole in the Sidewalk

Same Song, Second Verse, Same Theme

I

I walk down the street.

There is a deep hole in the sidewalk. I fall in.

I am lost . . . I am helpless.

It isn't my fault.

It takes forever to find a way out.

Kathryn is a homemaker. In spite of raising three daughters, she became bored as a homemaker and gradually found herself creating excuses to be in social circles where people drank, used cocaine, and partied. This led to outside sexual affairs. At the age of thirty-three, with her husband threatening to leave her if she did not stop her behavior, she sought treatment and began a recovery process.

II

I walk down the same street.

There is a deep hole in the sidewalk.

I pretend I don't see it.

I fall in again.

I can't believe I am in the same place

but it isn't my fault.

It still takes a long time to get out.

Kathryn was active in a recovery program for a couple of years. She enjoyed the fellowship, the women's meetings, and she had a sponsor. But she only shared at an intimate level with her sponsor. It was here she would talk, for the first time, about having been repeatedly sexually abused as a child. She gradually found herself becoming preoccupied with health issues and received a lot of attention for what seemed to be repetitive and severe health problems. Her first relapse occurred with prescription pain pills. After a year of actively using, she went through detox and once again sought out twelve-step programs.

III

I walk down the same street.
    There is a deep hole in the sidewalk. I see it is there.
    I still fall in . . . it's a habit.
    My eyes are open.
    I know where I am.
It is my fault.
I get out immediately.

For the next year and a half, Kathryn's recovery followed the same pattern as her first time around. She embraced the fellowship and the women in it, had the same sponsor with whom she would continue to talk about her sexual abuse, and once again became preoccupied with what appeared to be self-imposed health issues. She relapsed again. Three years later she detoxed again and returned to the same home group and sponsor.

Mark took a similar journey.

I

I walk down the street.
    There is a deep hole in the sidewalk. I fall in.
    I am lost . . . I am helpless.
    It isn't my fault.
It takes forever to find a way out.

Mark began his addictive behaviors as a teenager. His first treatment experience was just after high school graduation when his parents insisted he go. After treatment, he attended self-help meetings and liked them. He talked in meetings and was most verbal about his need for a job. When he got a job, his first goal was to buy a car—which he did within months. By this time he had fallen in love. In his mind, all was going great and then he relapsed. Within weeks, he lost his job, his girlfriend, and wrecked his uninsured car. His parents paid a second time to send him to treatment.

II

I walk down the same street.
    There is a deep hole in the sidewalk.
    I pretend I don't see it.
    I fall in again.
I can't believe I am in the same place

But it isn't my fault.
It still takes a long time to get out.

Mark was glad to be back with his recovery friends. He was chagrined about what happened and determined to not let that occur again. Within a month, he clearly needed a job and a car to get around. His friends heard about his remorse, his struggles with day-to-day living, and before long he had a job and a car. He met a young woman, and again, this was the love of his life. Aware of what happened last time, he knew he couldn't be complacent about his recovery. Yet, he became very busy, and after a time, he again relapsed.

III

I walk down the same street.
There is a deep hole in the sidewalk. I see it is there.
I still fall in . . . it's a habit.
My eyes are open.
I know where I am.
It is my fault.
I get out immediately.

No one saw Mark for a long time, until one day he showed up very distressed, just out of treatment for a third time. He went to a lot of meetings, talked about his remorse over relapsing, and expressed his gratitude for his parents who had once again paid for treatment. He was thankful for his friends; they helped him follow job leads and he met another woman. As much as he cared for this woman, when she became pregnant he was not sure what to do. This all began to feel familiar. Would he be able to make some changes before he started to use again?

To move from Chapter III to IV and V, it is important to identify repetitive relapse patterns. It is quite possible you are repeating behaviors that sabotage your recovery. The following are just some of the areas commonly involved in repeated relapses.

Choice of friends
Choice of sponsor
Participation in recovery meetings
How much you listen
Practice service work
Priorities
Behavior in relationships
Attitude, such as complacency, argumentativeness, impatience, etc.
What you are not discussing

A Hole in the Sidewalk

Identify the patterns of decision-making and behavior that put you at risk of relapse.

1) _____

2) _____

3) _____

4) _____

5) _____

6) _____

7) _____

8) _____

In asking addicts with various disorders what they needed to do differently to move from the third to the fourth and then to the fifth chapter of "A Hole in the Sidewalk," they identified:

Accept being an addict

Get a sponsor

Follow direction

Go to more meetings

Listen to others

Prioritize recovery over being in a relationship

Prioritize recovery over work

Stop going to places where they used or acted out

Limit and let go of certain relationships

Stop accepting family enabling

Dump emotional baggage

Tell the truth

Reach out for help even when not sure it is needed

Share both the good and the bad at meetings

Find ways to help others and not be so self-focused

Quit putting expectations on recovery

Identify what you see yourself doing differently that will allow you to get to Chapter V of "A Hole in the Sidewalk."

_____

_____

_____

_____

_____

_____

Let's conclude this journey with another look at Kathryn and Mark.

Kathryn came back to the same group and the same sponsor. When her sponsor suggested she see a psychotherapist to address her sexual abuse, she did. She identified her chronic use of prescription pills and its connection to her need to see doctors. She expanded her recovery program to include additional types of meetings. Willingness, a change in behavior, and insight led to her ability to walk around the hole in the sidewalk. Ultimately, she saw the need to walk down a different street.

Mark was about to become a father and knew that he needed to make some changes in his approach to recovery. He became less preoccupied with his love life, material gains, and the need to look good. He found himself wanting to talk at a deeper level with his sponsor and at meetings. He began hearing things differently than before. He sought out additional recovering friends. He took responsibility for allowing himself to be rescued by his parent's money, and began to pay them back. He began to walk around the hole, and while it would take more time, ultimately he would walk down a different street.

IV

I walk down the same street.
There is a deep hole in the sidewalk.
I walk around it.

V

I walk down another street.

Identify negative repetitious patterns

Identify constructive behaviors to support recovery

Today, I am grateful for _____

May you walk down a different street.

Resources

There are currently several million recovering people around the planet attending twelve-step meetings on a regular basis. It is relatively easy to find a meeting in any city or country if you know where to look. The internet provides access to information on a wide variety of recovery resources; these may change, so please check your search engines if the links do not work.

The following is a directory of twelve-step organizations.

Alcoholics Anonymous
Box 459 Grand Central Station
NYC, NY 10163
212.870.3400
www.alcoholics-anonymous.org

Alanon/Alateen
1600 Corporate Landing Pkwy
Virginia Beach, VA 23454
800.344.2666 (option #3) meeting info only
757.563.1600 / 888.4ALANON
www.al-anon.org
www.al-anon.org/alateen.html

Adult Children of Alcoholics
PO Box 3216
Torrance, CA 90510
310.534.1815
www.adultchildren.org

Co-dependents Anonymous
PO Box 670861 (meetings info)
Dallas, TX 75367-0861
706.648.6868 World Service Office
www.codependents.org

COSA (Co-Sex Addicts Anonymous)
National Services 612.537.6904
www.shore.net/cosa

Debtors Anonymous
PO Box 888 (World Services Office)
Needham, MA 02492-0009
781.453.2743
212.969.8111 (greater NY area)
www.debtorsanonymous.org

Eating Addictions Anonymous
www.dcregistry.com/users/eatingaddictions

Emotions Anonymous
www.emotionsanonymous.org

Families Anonymous
PO Box 3475
Culver City, CA 90231-3475
818.989.7841
800.736.9805
www.familiesanonymous.org

Gamblers Anonymous
PO Box 17173
Los Angeles, CA 90017
213.386.8789
www.gamblersanonymous.org

Marijuana Anonymous
www.marijuana-anonymous.org

Narcotics Anonymous
PO Box 9999
Van Nuys, California USA 91409
www.na.org

Cocaine Anonymous
PO Box 2000 (World Services Office)
Los Angeles, CA 90049-8000
310.559.5833
www.ca.org

Nat. Council on Alcoholism &
Drug Dependence
12 W 21st St
NYC, NY 10010
212.206.6770
www.ncadd.org

Nicotine Anonymous
www.nicotine-anonymous.org

Overeaters Anonymous
6075 Zenith Court
Rio Rancho, NM 87174
505.8912664
www.overeatersanonymous.org

Pills Anonymous
PO Box 772
Bronx, NY 10451
212.874.0700
http://club.yahoo.com/clubs/pillsanonymous

Rational Recovery System
Box 800
Lotus, CA 95651
530.621.4374
800.303.2873
www.rational.org/recovery

Recovering Couples Anonymous
PO Box 11872
St Louis, MO 63105
314.397.0867
www.recovering-couples.org

S-Anon
PO Box 111242
Nashville, TN 37222-1242
615.833.3152
www.sanon.org

National Assoc. for Children of Alcoholics
10920 Connecticut Ave Ste 100
Kensington MD 20895
888.554.2627
www.nacoa.org

Sex Addicts Anonymous
PO Box 70949
Houston, TX 77270
800.477.8191
www.sexaa.org

Sexaholics Anonymous (SA)
International Central Office
PO Box 300
Simi Valley, CA 93602
www.sa.org

Sexual Compulsives Anonymous (SCA)
West Coast
PO Box 4470
170 Sunset Blvd #520
Los Angeles, CA 90027
310.859.5585

East Coast
PO Box 1585
Old Chelsea Station
NYC, NY 10011
212.429.1123
www.sca-recovery.org

Sex & Love Addicts Anonymous (SLAA)
PO Box 338
Norwood, MA 02062-0338
781.255.8825
www.slaafws.org

Survivors of Incest Anonymous
PO Box 21817 (World Service Office)
Baltimore, MD 21222-6817
410.282.3400
www.siawso.org

Women for Sobriety & Men for Sobriety
PO Box 618
Quakertown, PA 18951
215.536.8026
www.womenforsobriety.org

Resources by Claudia Black, PhD

Books

Anger Strategies

Depression Strategies

Family Strategies

Relapse Toolkit

A Hole in the Sidewalk

Changing Course

Deceived

It Will Never Happen To Me

Intimate Treason

My Dad Loves Me, My Dad Has A Disease

Repeat After Me

Straight Talk

The Truth Begins With You

Unspoken Legacy

DVDs

Anger

Addiction in the Family

Breaking the Silence

Children of Denial

Double Jeopardy

Healing from Childhood Sexual Abuse

The History of Addiction

Issues of Recovery

The Legacy of Addiction

Relapse: Illusion of Immunity

Relationship Series

Triggering Effect

What Do I Say to My Kids?

CDs

A Time for Healing

Emotional Baggage

Imageries

Letting Go Imageries

Putting the Past Behind

Trauma in the Addicted Family

Triggers

To arrange a speaking engagement with Claudia Black, PhD, please contact

Claudja Inc.

206.842.6303 (Phone) • 206.842.6235 (Fax)

www.claudiablack.com